BRAIDS

250 PATTERNS FROM
JAPAN, PERU & BEYOND

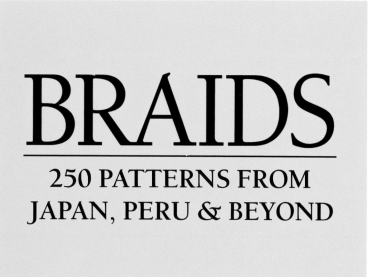

BRAIDS

250 PATTERNS FROM JAPAN, PERU & BEYOND

RODRICK OWEN

INTERWEAVE PRESS

This book is dedicated to
Sue, Megan and Steffan

U.S. edition:
Interweave Press, Inc.
201 East Fourth Street
Loveland, Colorado 80537

First published 1995 by Cassell
Villiers House, 41/47 Strand, London WC2N 5JE

ISBN 1-883010-06-3

Typeset by Method Limited, Epping, Essex, UK

Printed and bound in Singapore

Design
Gwyn Lewis
Illustrations and graphics
Ann Norman
Photography of individual braids and pages 11–14, 16, 17, 25, 31, 33, 38, 43 and 45
David Nutt
Jacket photography and pages 49, 71, 87, 99, 129 and 139
Ed Barber

Contents

Acknowledgements

I would like to thank a wonderful group of friends who, together, have given up hours of their time. I dare not add up the number of hours: Ann Nutt, Lizzie Cook and Christine Wrigley, who made hundreds of samples to test the instructions; Ernie Henshall for sharing his two-braid designs, numbers 3 and 53, and for his method of making braids using the slotted-board method; David Nutt, who spent a long time on his knees taking photographs; Ann Norman for drawing the illustrations again and again; Ralph Norman, who designed the graphics with his computer fingers; the wordsmiths Shirley Berlin, Ken Winter and Ann Norman, who read the manuscript and gave helpful suggestions.

My special thanks also go to Ralph Norman for his editorial skills and support.

I would also like to thank Jill Owen, who has spent hours typing and pasting up.

My thanks also go to the Winston Churchill Memorial Trust for giving me the opportunity to study in Japan, and to my *sensei* in Tokyo, Makiko Tada, for her generous teaching and for giving permission to use the *sohbi*-style notation for the Japanese braid designs.

Thanks also to Adele Cahlander, Esther Warner Dendel, Alta Turner, Noemi Speiser and Jack Lenor Larsen, whose works have all been, in their own way, an inspiration for me to complete this book; and to two people who started me on a journey back in 1979: Pat Moloney at the London College of Furniture, who encouraged me to work in textiles, and Mary Frame, who introduced me to the world of braids.

Introduction

The further up and the further in you go, the bigger everything gets. The inside is larger than the outside. Like an onion: except that as you go in and in, each circle is larger than the last.   Tales of Narnia, C.S. Lewis

The rope braids in this book have been chosen for three reasons. First, the braids of Peru and Japan have more beautiful surface patterns and more varied structures than those of other countries. Second, all these designs can be made on equipment that is readily available and easy to use. Third, these braids have many applications, both old and new, decorative and functional.

Some of the braids in this book can be taught in a few minutes to children as young as six years old; yet ancient patterns can produce braids so complex that textile researchers are still trying to understand them.

Making braids is always exciting. When you have chosen the fibres, colours and patterns, waiting for the first glimpse of the emerging braid is always a moment of anticipation. But beware, braid-making can be addictive.

'What do you do with braids?' may be a question that has no real answer. As soon as one is asked to write down ideas on how to use braids, the mind tends to shut down. However, if one thinks of general areas of use, answers flow a little easier.

A group at the Textile Arts Festival (Bradford, 1990) came up with these areas of practical applications: fashion: jewellery, belts, handles and trims for clothing; interior design: trimmings, tie backs and pulls; ecclesiastical: stoles, borders for garments and altars, and hangings; and equestrian: many sorts of braids can be used for harness and trappings. When they were asked 'Why do you make braids? What do they mean to you?' The group gave the following reasons, which may be the right place for everyone to start: a braid is a personal expression; it is an ornament; it can be used for embellishment. A braid is a universal symbol. Braids are movement; they are alive. Braids are beautiful; they are sensual; they are intense; they are dense; they have a jewel-like quality. The colour is intense. Braids are completeness. Concentration is needed to make a braid. They are a meditation; they are harmony. While you are making a braid, you give life to the threads.

Holding a length of finished braid in your hand, feeling its weight, its drape, watching the colours and feeling the sensual movement as it is drawn through the fingers from one hand to the other, give an inner answer to the question why the braid has been made. It is an expression of inner meaning, it has been a personal journey – from crossing and arranging the threads, through the process of making, watching the braid as it slowly grows in length and, at the end, a feeling of completeness.

Many people who make braids enjoy the direct contact with the threads and the calming experience that the act of braiding brings. Some people, indeed, are quite content to make lots of samples just for the sheer pleasure.

Whatever your reason for making braids, remember that this book, or any book, is only the continuation of the journey. Braiding is eternally fascinating, and always open to new discoveries. The aim of this book is to provide an introduction to braids and braiding so that many more may come to share in these skills.

After a brief look at the history of braids, therefore, the book is divided into two main sections. The first section describes the basic materials, equipment and methods needed to construct braids. These range from a braiding stool (the traditional Maru Dai of Japan), through adaptations of this to other equipment, which is simply constructed from easily obtained materials.

The second section covers braid design. This subject is too wide to be covered fully in a single book, so the designs here are confined to those that have a rope-like appearance; they are round, square, flat and hollow. The patterns mainly originate from Peruvian designs, but a few from Japan are also included, as are some seafaring braids. A dual system for making each design is given, either on a braiding stool, a Maru Dai, or on a small piece of card. The designs progress from simple 4-strand patterns through 8 and 16 strands to 24-strand patterns. The final design in the book has 31 strands. The reader is taken through the designs, building on skills learnt from the first two designs.

The book ends with a brief discussion of the relationship between braids and mathematics, and how this might be used in schools.

History

Braids must have had a universal awakening. Two strands twisted together for strength would have developed into 3- and 4-strand braids used as early tools in hunting and gathering communities. Later, straps, belts, slings and baskets made from plant fibres appeared as solutions to practical problems. The knowledge of dyes and the use of animal fibres led to designs with more complex structures and to new applications, such as adornment, and examples of this increased complexity can be seen in the ancient braids from Peru and Japan.

Having come into being out of a need, braids became important in their own right. They were regarded as symbols of power, valued adjuncts to ritual and ceremony and imbued with meaning. In ancient Peru turbans, slings and braids for tassels were used in burial ceremonies, along with wrapped/braided reeds and gods' eyes. In Japan braids were used in the rituals of Buddhism to edge and secure religious scrolls. Certain colours are used as a means of protection during what are considered the unlucky years. In ancient Italy and Spain interlaced braids were used as a protection against witches and the evil eye.

W.L. Hildburgh, writing in 1944, noted that: 'When a family is afraid of witchery, they should undertake some kind of *lavori intereciati* (braided work), for witches cannot enter a house where there is anything of the kind hung up – so in making garments of any kind for men or women they should include interlaced braids or stitches, for when the witches see such interlacing they can do nothing because they cannot count the threads nor stitches.'

Another example of interlaced protection comes from Italy: 'When a peasant prunes the mulberry trees which are for silk worms, he must trim them so that the boughs *restino intereciati* (may remain interlaced), in which case the silkworms will be protected against any *malocchio* (evil influences of witches).'

Beaded chiefs' costumes from Nigeria have the same appearance as some Peruvian structures and are reminiscent of the Yin Yang interlacing from Japan. These are echoed in the Celtic interlacing found engraved in stone and as painted ornamentation in illuminated manuscripts. Braids are universal and powerful symbols, indeed.

Peruvian and Japanese braids developed quite independently of each other, each country not only producing its own unique designs but also working with different fibres and methods. After a period of using vegetable fibres, Peruvians used cotton, llama, alpaca and, today, wool and synthetic yarns. Japanese braiders moved from vegetable fibres to silk, and now use a rayon, known as biron, as a silk substitute.

Each country's methods of constructing braids are also quite different. Today in Peru braids are made in the hand, probably in the same way as in the past. In Japan, on the other hand, various wooden devices are used to support braiding structures, which would have been made by a hand-held loop method in earlier times.

Peruvian Sling Braids

A sling is a weapon made from a length of braid. At the centre of the braid is a pouch in which a missile is placed. By swinging the sling in a wide circle and letting go of one end, a missile can be projected over a long distance with great force. The sling is by no means peculiar to Peru – it was also known in Africa, India and Tibet, the Far East and throughout the islands of the Pacific Ocean. Slings are known also to have been used in Europe and the Near East from the Bronze Age until the 17th century. Slings, whose missiles could outdistance arrows, were in regular use as long-range weapons, and they were also used throughout history to keep unwelcome predators away when herding animals.

Tibetan and Peruvian slings are made in the same way – that is, by holding and manipulating the threads in the hand. Although Tibetan slings are made with surface patterns, the Peruvian and Bolivian cultures have produced the most intricately designed slings.

The history of braids in Peru is elusive and can be discussed only in the context of mainstream textiles, and by relating them to finds at excavated sites, for Peruvian cultures did not have any form of written text.

Andean fabrics did not begin to appear in the western world until the mid-19th century. In 1874 William H. Holmes referred to a mummy pack and to the burial grounds of Ancon near Lima and to other sites up and down the coast of Peru. Among the textiles he examined were slings 'made from raw hide and cords', and he noted that 'they were braided in coloured wools in the most tasteful manner imaginable'. Although there was some awareness in western circles at the end of the 19th century, it was not until 1930–1950 that the museums of the world began to take a real interest. The study of Andean textiles is not very old compared with the work on Roman, Greek or Egyptian cultures.

PRE-CERAMIC CULTURE

Most civilizations have gone through a process of using vegetable fibres to make simple looped, twined and netted structures. Tapestry and network fragments that have been carbon-dated to 8600–5780BC were found in the Guitarrero caves in the northern highlands of Peru. It is suggested that this ability to make twined structures would have also included the skill to make rope by twisting strands together, and a natural consequence of this would be the manipulation of three and four strands together to make the first braids.

Further fabrics were discovered at a site in the Omas valley on the south coast. The finds consisted of over 300 funerary fabrics, dated to approximately 2000BC. These included plain cloth with feathers attached and bags made from simple looping or knotting. On the north coast, at Huaca Prieta in the Chimu Valley, some 2,700 textiles were excavated from a refuse midden of a village site. These fragments were cast-offs, made from cotton and bast fibres. When the structures were analysed it was found that 78 per cent of the textiles were twined, 10 per cent were looped and the remaining 12 per cent were made by various nettings. The twined fabrics were patterned, showing snakes, birds, crabs and other designs. These fabrics were dated at 2125–950BC.

CHAVIN

Evidence of the Chavin culture, which flourished c.1500–600BC, is preserved in the decorated stones in the ruins of their temples, and also in artefacts of wood, gold, silver and ceramics. Unfortunately, little has survived in the way of textiles. Some of those that have been found consist of fine woven fabrics, which were dyed with tannins from various trees. They depict deities such as puma-type figures and its feline god.

PARACAS – NAZCA

Evacuations on the dry sandy Paracas Peninsula revealed some 450 mummy bundles from two sites, known as Cavernas and Necropolis. Some of these mummies were as much as 1.2m (4ft) high by 1.7m (5ft 6in) in diameter. The outer wrapping of the mummy consisted of plain cotton cloth about 4m (13ft) wide and up to 20m (65ft) long. This fabric helped to protect the decorated fabrics that lay inside. Within each mummy bundle various artefacts were found, such as spinning spindles, headbands, fans, slings and other textiles. Slings held in museum collections that are referred to as Nazca could have come from this or from similar sites. Raoul D'Harcourt gives directions of how to make two slings from the Nazca period (900BC–AD650), and if complex structured slings were made during this period, it seems reasonable that simple 8- and 16-strand slings could have been made in the pre-ceramic culture too.

HUARI CULTURE

The Huari people, who lived from c.300 to 900, established a religion and social organization centred on Tiahuanaco, now in Bolivia. Huari textiles are known for their beautiful tapestry woven shirts, which depicted a deity with a feline's head and falcon's wings. This design eventually developed from a realistic style to a stylized, geometric design, which could be a modern design from our own time. It has been suggested that the textiles were produced by organized craftsmen, making to a certain size and quality.

The Chimu culture (900–1500) and the Chancay culture (900–1600) did not produce textiles of particular note. The fabrics were loosely woven, probably on back-strap looms.

A sling from Tibet. As in Peru, Tibetan sling-makers work with the braid held in the fist.

INCA CULTURE

The strength of the Inca discipline on the people dominated the creative skills of the crafts. During this period (1300–1532) textile designs became geometric and excluded anything organic, while the production was organized, with women called upon to weave fabrics in special workshops, producing clothes probably intended for military use. In addition, there were workshops that wove sumptuous clothes for the Inca and his wives. The garments were made from llama and vicuna wools, which were dyed with bright colours and decorated with gold discs and feathers.

In 1532 the highly organized military weight of the Inca empire fell to 200 Spaniards led by Francisco Pizarro, thus bringing an end to the natural Peruvian culture. During the early years of the Conquest, a Spanish observer wrote: 'Their chief weapon is the sling. With it they can throw a large stone with such force that it could kill a horse. I have seen a stone flung from 30 paces break in two a sword that a man was holding in his hand.'

SLING BRAIDS TODAY

Sling braids presumably continue to be made today, in the same way that they were in past. The main uses today are for herding and ceremonial occasions. Sling-making has traditionally been a man's skill and, although women can make slings, they choose not to. Braiders prefer to use alpaca for ceremonial slings, and they will spin their own yarn before commencing to braid. They will use llama for herding slings.

Regional variations in sling-making exist throughout Peru. The finest examples come from Hauncavelica, where core-carrying braids with diamond designs are made. Animals, lizards and writing are portrayed along the length of the braid. Ceremonial rope braids are also made without pouches. These are decorated with tassels and short braids, which are attached along the length. They are called Wuyfala and are used by the men at the carnivals.

It is from this background that the sling braid designs in this book have been chosen.

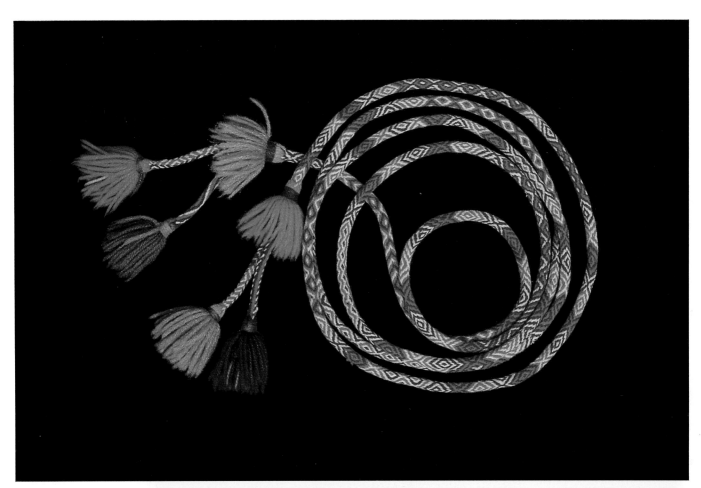

Known as a Simpita, this three-coloured braid has been made with various changes of pattern along its length. Simpitas originate from the Ayacucho area of Peru, and when they are worn by unmarried women they are known as Para Solteras.

This contemporary dance tassel, from the Cuzco area of Peru, is a complex, five-colour braid known as a Wichi-Wichi.

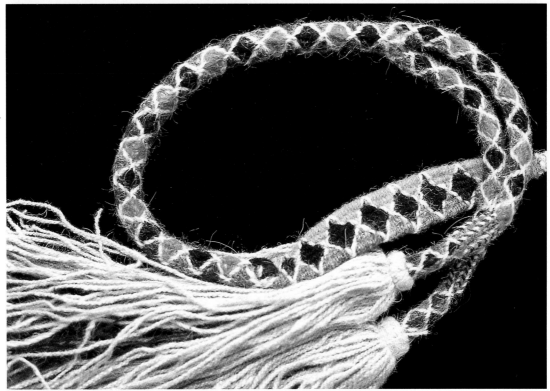

Japanese Kumihimo

The word Kumihimo means 'the gathering of threads', and it is a general word applied to braiding.

Four basic pieces of equipment are used in Japan today:

Maru Dai (round stand) – this piece of equipment is used to make the braids described in this book.

Kaku Dai (square stand) – this is used to make a round braid with a high lustre. The braids grow up from the device and are made around different shaped spigots.

Aya Take Dai (low stand) – this equipment makes flat braids with a twined structure and uses separate weft threads. It is similar to tablet weaving.

Taka Dai (high stand) – this makes flat braids with a twill structure, either single or double layered.

Japanese history is divided into conveniently defined and dated periods, and an abundance of information is available on social and political events. However, the history of Kumihimo is sparse, not only because it is one of the backwaters of textile tradition but also because much information was kept secret and passed down orally. Even today much information on braiding, particularly on the Taka Dai, is closely guarded.

A dance sling, probably from the Cuzco area of Peru, with coloured pompons that have been made separately and stitched onto the braid.

JOMON AND YAYOI

The earliest periods of Japanese history are the Jomon (8000–400BC) and the Yayoi (400BC–AD300). Little evidence remains from these eras from which we can draw firm conclusions about the type of braid that might have been made. This is not surprising in a climate with high humidity, because natural fibres quickly decompose. It is known from pieces of clay pots that twisted ropes were pressed into the clay to make patterns. The word Jomon means 'rope pattern', and many of the impressions made and overlaid on the pottery indicate that they represent braided structures. These early twisted ropes and braids would have been made from plant fibres, and they echo similar textile development in other early cultures around the world.

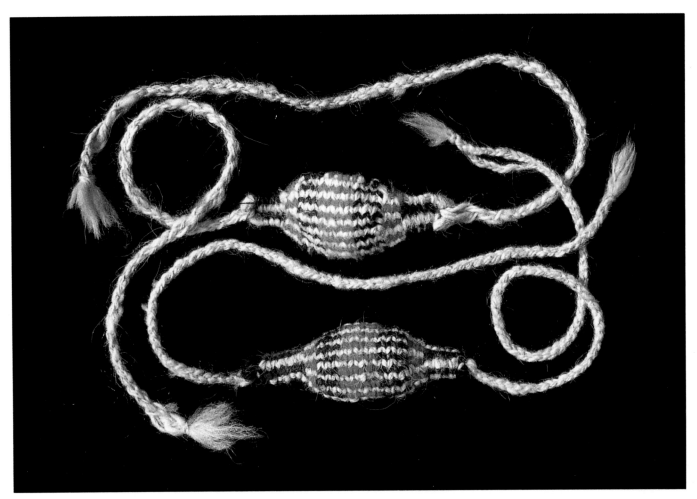

KOFUN

During the Kofun era (300–500) huge burial mounds, Kofun, were built to bury important leaders. It is from these tombs that the Haniwa pottery figures were excavated. The figures are dressed in ceremonial clothes and are adorned with cords, which are used as belts, garment closures and hair ties.

In her booklet on Kumihimo, Makiko Tada refers to a report of a bronze mirror that was found buried at Kunesam in the Iga prefecture. The mirror was partly covered with what appeared to be a square vermilion braid. It is unfortunate that the braid has not survived for us to see.

ASUKA

In the Asuka era (552–645) the king of the Korean kingdom of Packche urged the Japanese emperor to embrace Buddhism. At first the arrival of Buddhist practice in Japan was seen as a threat to the ruling classes and caused great civil unrest, but when the disputes were eventually resolved, Buddhism was absorbed into Japanese social and political life.

These two braided slings from Palestine may be very similar to ones that were used in Old Testament times.

The Buddhist religion brought with it sutras and scrolls, which were trimmed and tied with braids and, as the religion spread, the need for braids grew. It is not known how or where these braids were made – they may have been imported from Korea and China or made in Japan.

Early wall paintings in the tomb Takamatsu–Zuka near Nara depict men and women in clothes adorned with braids. The style of dress shows that at this period Korean influence on Japanese society was still strong.

NARA

The Shoso-in museum at Nara stores many artefacts from this period (645–784), including fragments of braids, and it is from these original structures that the braids of today have been developed. Braids continued to be used for religious ceremonies, but they were also used as ties to secure pendants, mirrors and so on, and they were used as bag ties and for tying knots, Musubi.

Braids made from the Shoso-in colours – lilac, purple, blue, green, gold and Chinese orange – were introduced from China for use in Kumihimo. At this time those colours were used to ward off evil spirits, and it is still the custom in Japan that there are unlucky years in a person's life: 25 and 42 for men and 19 and 33 for women. It is said that if women use a braid with Shoso-in colours they will avoid misfortune, and even today in Kyoto and some other regions people still observe this custom.

HEIAN

The Heian period (784–1184) saw great Buddhist influence in all aspects of life. The temples employed many artists and craftsmen who produced work of outstanding beauty, and during this time braids became truly Japanese, complex in structure and sophisticated in design.

Two styles of braids emerged, the first being the Hirao sash, a wide, flat, supple braid, made with plied silk. This braid, which was developed from the Sazanami chevron design from China and became known as Karakumi, was worn by the Emperor and high-ranking officials. It was between 15 and 25cm (6-10in) wide. The edges were usually made up of a diamond design, while the centre panel was space-dyed and decorated with embroidered birds and flowers. The braid was tied around the waist, the long tasselled ends hanging down the front of the body.

The second group of braids, designated as temple braids because they were discovered hidden inside statues in the temples, are rope braids. They are named after the temples where the fragments were found. The braids are core-carrying and resemble the Peruvian core braids. An example is Saidai-ji, which is made with 56 bobbins. Others are Chuzon-ji and Choin-in, and Shitennoji, which can be made with up to 172 bobbins. A flat temple braid was found at the Itsukushima shrine on Miyajima Island.

Writing in the Textile Museum Journal in 1986, Masako Kinoshita describes her research into hand-looped braids that used a foot-beating device, Ashiuchi No Himo, to tighten the braid as it was worked. It is more than possible that loop-manipulated braids were being made as early as the seventh century. Today, reconstructions of the temple braids are made on wooden devices that are known as Dai Maru Dai.

Opposite A traditional Maru Dai with 16 bobbins. The Maru Dai is the most widely used piece of braiding equipment.

KAMAKURA – MUROMACHI

The rise of the Samurai warrior in the Kamakura (1185–1333) and Muromachi (1333–1573) periods created a demand for armour, and, as this was made up from a large number of small plates laced together with braids, Kumihimo was also in demand. The Kumihimo was made as strong, flexible, flat braid in 2.5m (approximately 8ft) lengths, and some 250–300m (800–1,000ft) were required for each suit of armour. As the demand for braiding grew, quicker methods of production had to be found. One method was hand looping, which was quicker than the Taka Dai. Another was the invention of the Aya Taka Dai, a device that makes braids with a twined structure. At this time braids were also made for sword hilts, leggings and horse harnesses. The braids for lacing the armour were usually of one plain colour, while the braids for swords and for edging parts of the armour were patterned. The pattern favoured by the Samurai to secure his sword to his body is called Kikko design, a hexagonal-shaped pattern representing the hard shell of the tortoise. Kikko is the symbol for long life.

As Japan settled into a time of peace, the Samurai became more involved in matters of state and, influenced by Zen Buddhism, turned their attention to aesthetic pursuits. It was during this time that the art of the tea ceremony emerged, and braids came to be used as edgings for covers and scrolls, as well as for attachments to the tea utensils.

MONOYAMA – EDO

The Monoyama period (1573–1614) saw the appearance of the Nagoya obi, a broad, round braid with tassels, which was tied at the back of the kimono in a bow. A narrow braid, an obijama, was tied over the obi to stop it from slipping. This was the beginning of the braiding that is used in Japan today.

The Edo period (1616–1867) was a time of peace but not of great artistic note, a reflection of the conservative nature of the ruling shoguns. However, during this time braids were also used as ties, made to join netsuke (small carved toggles) to inro (small tiered cases), which were secured to the waist sash.

The late Edo period was probably when the Taka Dai, as it is known today, was introduced, making it possible to produce braids of various chequered patterns in plain and twill structures. Edo (Tokyo) became the focal point of Kumihimo, and early published works in the form of sample books of braids originate from here.

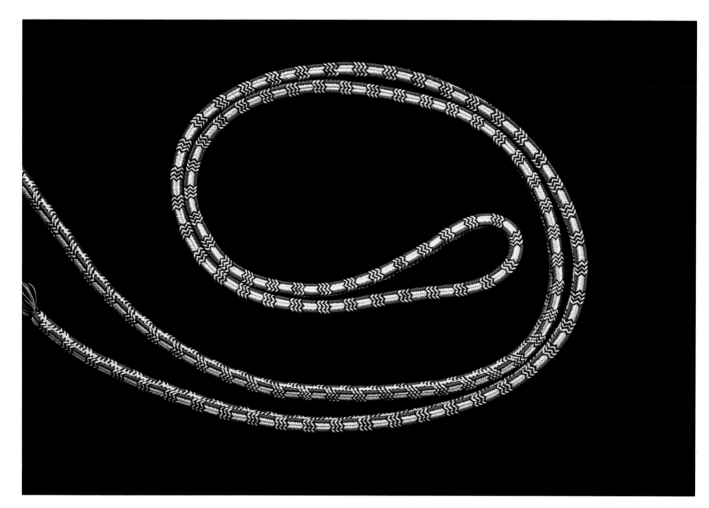

MEIJI – TAISHO – SHOWA

The Meiji period (1867–1912) saw great social changes. In 1876 an order to prohibit the carrying of swords was issued, and also at this time machines were introduced to make Kumihimo. Both these factors affected the demand for hand-made Kumihimo.

In the late Meiji period the Taka Dai was further developed to make braids constructed on two and even three levels, enabling braiders to make braid with non-repeating patterns (Ayadashi braids) – a form of double cloth made by twill weaving with pick-up patterns.

In the mid-1970s books of instructions on making braids using the Maru Dai and Kaku Dai began to appear. Schools to teach braid-making were established and attracted many students who were interested in the continuance of the traditional art of Kumihimo in Japan.

It still remains for comprehensive information to be published on how to make braids on the Aya Taka Dai and the Taka Dai.

Shown here is a reproduction of an original Japanese 14th-century braid. It is named Saidai-ji, after the temple in which it was discovered, and it was made with 56 bobbins.

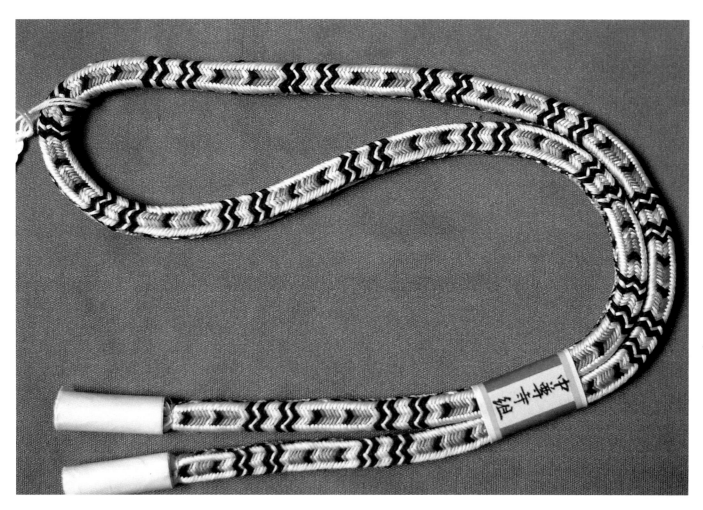

A 14th-century Chuzon-ji, another ancient temple braid from
Japan. This braid can be made with either 72 or 144 bobbins.

Equipment, Materials and Methods

This chapter introduces the different devices that can be used to make braids, both by the absolute beginner and by those with more experience.

There are four methods to consider. The first is the traditional Japanese braiding stool called a Maru Dai. The second is an easy-to-make Maru Dai, constructed from cardboard. The third is a series of slotted pieces of cardboard, three square and three round. These are held in the hand and are near to the way braids are made in Peru, over the hand without any devices. The fourth method is a small wooden stand, which supports a slotted board and uses weights similar to the Maru Dai.

Metric and Imperial Measurements

The measurements of length and weight that are shown in this book are given in metric. In the case of lengths, the metric measure is followed by the approximate imperial equivalent. This is not, however, the case with weights. The weights of bobbins and counterbalances are given in metric only, for these weights represent a world standard set by the Japanese system of braid-making that is referred to in all Japanese and English publications.

An understanding of weights is critical to braid-making, and the knowledge is of benefit when accessing other publications for further designs. Equipment suppliers in the UK, Canada and USA all supply in gram weights (see Suppliers).

The simple formula for converting grams to ounces is to multiply the gram weight by 0.0353. If you need to convert ounces to grams, multiply the ounce weight by 28.350.

Equipment

THE BRAIDING STOOL – MARU DAI

The Maru Dai is a wooden stool. It has a round top with a hole in the centre, four legs and a base, which is usually square. The top of the Maru Dai shown in this book is 250mm (10in) in diameter, which is suitable for making braids of up to 36 strands, using bobbins of 100gm or less. The overall height is 420mm (16½in); the base is 250mm (10in) square.

The top is made of a close-grained wood, such as sycamore, cherry or maple. The finish on all parts should be smooth. The legs and the base can be sanded down and coated with a wood sealer, but the top should be left untreated. If it is sealed, the threads will slip and will be more difficult to control. The natural friction of the threads as they are moved around the Maru Dai will gradually give the top a matured smoothness.

The top of the Maru Dai is called kagami, which means mirror. The mirror is seen to reflect the quality of the braid as it is made and, therefore, the braid-maker. On no account should anything be placed on the mirror. Any indentation, however slight, will affect the quality of the work and muddy the reflection.

Do not allow the top of your Maru Dai to become damp or wet, for this will raise the grain and it will become rough. If this does happen, the top can be restored to a smooth finish by carefully rubbing down the wood following the direction of the grain with a grade 00 flour paper, fine sandpaper or fine steel wool (grade 0000).

Maru in the context of Kumihimo means round. There is, however, an older use of the word. Laurens Van der Post in his book *Portrait of Japan* writes: 'It was a special word the Japanese had for expressing the mystique of their relationship with the things they fashioned according to some image of their spirit.' This, of course, applies not only to Kumihimo but also to the many other skills that are affected by those essential moments of energy, between our centre and fingertips that creates that which is shibui. There does not appear to be a direct translation of the word shibui. It concerns that which has a profound essence. More about this philosophy can be read in *The Unknown Craftsman: A Japanese insight into beauty* by Soetsu Yanagi, adapted by Bernard Leach.

BOBBINS

The Japanese name for bobbin is tama. In early times bobbins were made of clay, and their shape was reminiscent of a diabolo or dumb-bell; today bobbins are made from wood.

Each braiding school has designed its own bobbin shape with preferred bobbin weights. The bobbins are made from close-grained wood with a metal insert to give the necessary weight.

The old Japanese units of measurement went out of use more than a decade ago, but they are still used by braiders. For example, the sizes of Maru Dais are referred to in units of *sun*. A sun is a unit of 30.3mm (1³⁄₁₆in) in length. The 250mm (10in) mirror is equivalent to an 8 sun Maru Dai, 242mm (9½in).

The bobbins are measured in *momme*; one momme is equal to 3.75gm. The information shown in the table below was collected from various sources. It indicates the different weights of bobbins available today in Japan. The bobbins marked with an asterisk are made in the UK and are readily available (see Suppliers).

		*	*		*			*	
MOMME	10	18	22.5	26.6	30	40	64	70	200
GRAM	35	70	83.5	100	112.5	150	240	262.5	750

Bobbin Ties

The tie is the link between the bobbin and the end of the thread. Its purpose is to act as an extension to the warp, allowing the braid to be made to its full length, leaving sufficient loose ends for a tassel.

Each bobbin will require a tie (see Figs. 1a, 1b and 1c).

1 Select and cut a fine plied cotton yarn 900mm (35in) long.

2 Fold it in half and tie an overhand knot with the loose ends and pull tight (Fig. 1a).

Fig. 1a

3 With the knotted end of the tie form a larkshead knot (Fig. 1b).

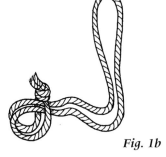
Fig. 1b

4 Slip the larkshead knot around the waist of the bobbin and pull tight (Fig. 1c).

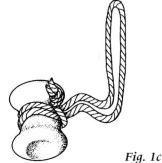
Fig. 1c

COUNTERBALANCE WEIGHTS

The counterbalance pulls the braided warp down through the centre hole (Fig. 2). In Japan counterbalance weights are called *omori*. The most common is a system of metal discs, with a choice of two systems using 90gm or 190gm weights. The discs are held in a small bag, which is attached to the braid on the underside of the Maru Dai.

Fishing weights make a good substitute for metal discs, and they are available in a convenient variety of shapes and sizes from 14gm to 225gm.

As a guide, the counterbalance should be about 45 per cent of the total bobbin weight. It should be noted that the heavier the counterbalance the looser the braid structure will be; a lighter counterbalance will give a tighter braid structure.

Counterbalance and Tension

Braids can be planned – the designs can be drafted on graph paper and the counterbalance can be calculated to give an

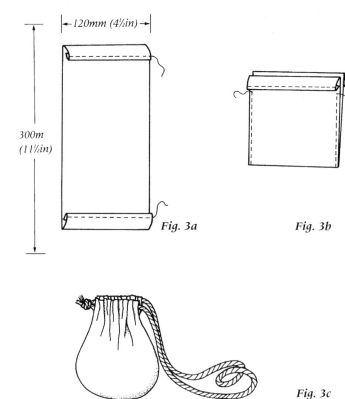

Fig. 2

Fig. 3a

Fig. 3b

Fig. 3c

expected braid tension in relation to the bobbins used.

There are, however, hidden factors to take into account. As in all design work, it pays to make samples. While you do so, adjustments can be made until you obtain a satisfactory result. Keep a record of the work and label all your samples. Everything to do with tensioning a braid is the interaction of calculations, skills and intuition.

The calculations are the measured relationship between bobbin and counterbalance weights and the thickness of the threads.

The skills are to do with experience. They are concerned with reading patterns; understanding which bobbins to move and where and how to reposition them; and knowing how to pick up the threads and to let them slip through the hands with a smooth movement.

Intuition is knowing. It is not easy to define, but it involves, for example, left- and right-hand balance, the correct amount of pressure, the rhythm and touch. In short, being able to forget what you know – because you know it.

The Counterbalance Bag

The bag for the counterbalance is made from cloth with a drawstring. You can make one to the following instructions.

1 Cut out a piece of fabric 300 × 120mm (11½ × 4½in).

2 Turn over and hem the two short sides, allowing sufficient room for the drawstring (Fig. 3a).

3 Fold in half and stitch sides (Fig. 3b). Do not oversew the drawstring hems. Turn inside out.

4 Either braid your own drawstring or use a length of soft cotton or nylon cord. Cut the cord 450mm (17½in) long.

5 Thread the drawstring through the top hems and tie the loose ends with an overhand knot. Pull the knotted end to the side of the bag (Fig. 3c).

Materials

There really is no limit to the yarns that can be used. Experiment with cotton, linen, mohair, cashmere, llama, alpaca, chenille, wool or synthetics, but remember that the choice of yarn should relate to the effect required.

Remember to record the following variables when the braid is finished. These factors seem so memorable when the braid is new but are irritatingly elusive when you try to replicate the same result later.

* name/number of design
* number/weight of bobbins
* the number and thickness of threads used for each bobbin
* counterbalance weight
* yarn used
* length of warp
* finished lengths and size

Fig. 3a caption label: ←120mm (4½in)→, 300m (11½in)

SILK AND BIRON THREADS

In Japan today, two main fibres are used to make Kumihimo – silk and biron, which is a type of rayon that has been specially designed to simulate silk. Other synthetic fibres are used, although to a lesser extent, together with metallic threads.

It is unusual to find a non-processed pure silk thread. The best non-processed silk has a 20 per cent filler added to prevent yellowing and to act as an insect repellent. Most silk thread supplied to make braids is to a count of approximately 150/3, known as 21chu. One 150/3 thread is made by spinning 21 silkworm threads together. Finer count threads of 12–14chu are available, and these are the threads that are used to make silk fabric for kimonos and western clothes and to make into the fine silk squares used by magicians.

The round 21chu obijima braid that is tied over the obi when a kimono is worn should be made to a consistent thickness throughout its entire length. A standard 21chu braid is made from 672 individual 150/3 threads, and the number of threads per bobbin can be calculated by dividing the number of bobbins to be used into this figure. A round braid of 672 threads will be approximately 5–8mm (¼–⅜in) in diameter.

Much of the silk/biron used for braiding in Japan is sold in packets with pre-prepared warps. The warps are cut to length and divided into separate ropes. For example, a warp for a 16-strand braid will be cut into lengths of 2.7m (approximately 9ft) and divided into 16 separate ropes, each rope containing 42 ends of silk (39 for biron). The pre-prepared packets are available in the UK (see Suppliers).

The length of braid made from these cut warps varies between 1.4m (4ft 6in) and 1.7m (5ft 6in) according to the design and tension. There is on average a 40 per cent take-up on the cut length of the warp.

The above information can act as a benchmark for other fibres used, and the table below can be used as a guide to help you decide on bobbin weight and to calculate the number of threads per bobbin.

Warp Preparation for the Maru Dai

It is suggested that at first you begin with warps cut from yarns other than silk and that the warp is cut to twice the length of the required finished braid. Your experience and records will guide future allowances.

Four types of braid 'endings' are described: tasselled ends, wrapped-loop ends, braided-loop ends and finger-point ends. The basic warp preparation is the same for all four, but the final dressing of Maru Dai is slightly different for each. The complete sequence for tasselled ends is described, followed by the variations for the other three endings.

TABLE FOR 150/3 (21CHU) SILK

Number Bobbins per Braid	Standard Braid 672 Ends		Half Size Braid 336 Ends		Quarter Size Braid 168 Ends		Fine Braid 84 Ends	
	Ends per Bobbin	Bobbin size (grms)	Ends per Bobbin	Bobbin size (grms)	Ends per Bobbin	Bobbin size (grms)	Ends per Bobbin	Bobbin size (grms)
4	168	750	84	240	42	100	21	100
8	84	240	42	100	21	100	11	70
12	56	240	28	100	14	70/100	7	35/70
16	42	100	21	100	11	70	5	35
24	28	100	14	70/100	7	35/70	3	35
32	21	100	10	70	5	35	–	–
36	18	100	9	70	4	35	–	–

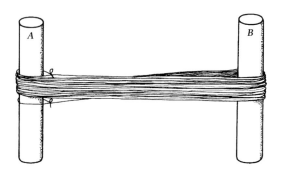

Fig. 4a

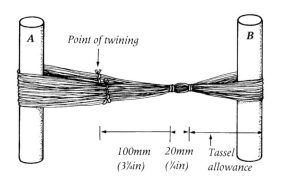

Fig. 4b

Fig. 4c

Fig. 4d

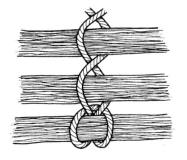

Fig. 4e

TASSELLED END PREPARATION

1 Select the braid to be made, then decide on the total length of the braid, allowing for tassels, and the number of threads per bobbin.

2 Before assembling the warping posts and beginning the circular warp (shown in Fig. 4a), calculate the total distance from post B to the 'point of twining' (as shown in Fig. 4b).

3 The stages of separating and twining the warp are shown in Figs. 4c, 4d and 4e.

Dressing the Maru Dai for Tasselled End

1 Cut the warp at post A, then thread the tassel end down through the centre hole, placing the twined warp over the top of the Maru Dai (Fig. 5a).

2 Insert a knitting needle through the warp between the two tied-off points and pull the loose warp upwards to bring the needle tight up to the underside of the Maru Dai (Fig. 5b). The warp is now ready to connect to the bobbin ties.

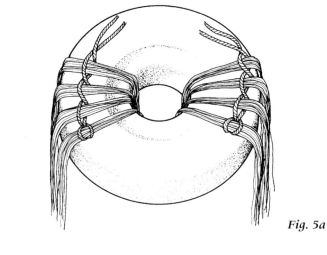

Fig. 5a

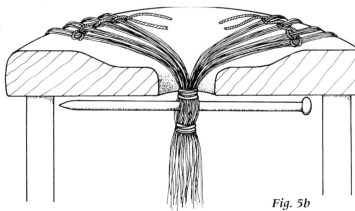

Fig. 5b

Before connecting the warp to the bobbin tie, care must be given to preparing the warp ends for each bobbin. In Japan this preparation is called *ito sabaki*, which means 'to govern the spirit in the thread' or 'to give life to the thread'. In practice it means separating the warp for each bobbin from the twined ends and stroking the threads along their full length (rather like brushing out long hair), until the threads lie smoothly together, side by side.

LOOPED AND FINGER-POINT ENDS

There are two looped-end beginnings. One is wrapped, the other is braided. The finger-point end is a braid with a round, blunt end. The preparation shown below is the same for all three.

1   Make a circular warp between the warping posts as shown in Fig 4a.
2   Separate the tied-off warp, counting out the threads per bobbin. Secure each group of threads by continuously twining at a point approximately 100mm (3¾in) from the larkshead knot at post B. The stages of separating and twining the warp are shown in Figs. 4c, 4d and 4e.
3   Cut a piece of yarn 400mm (15½in) long and fold it in half. Slip the looped end through the warp at post B, make a larkshead knot and pull it tight. Tie an overhand knot in the loose ends 30mm (1¼in) from post B (Fig. 6).

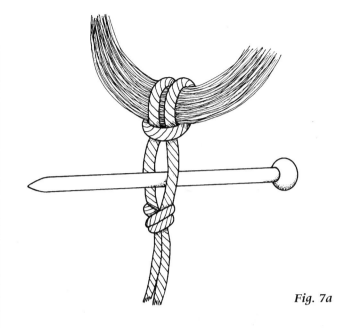

Fig. 7a

Dressing the Maru Dai for Finger-point End
Thread the warp down through the centre hole of the Maru Dai and insert a knitting needle into the 30mm (1¼in) loop, pulling the loose warp to bring the needle up tight to the underside of the Maru Dai (Figs. 7a and 7b). The warp is now ready to connect to the bobbin ties.

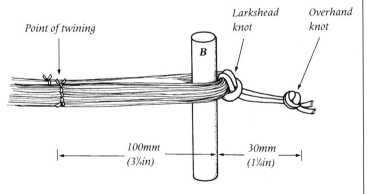

Point of twining

Larkshead knot

Overhand knot

B

100mm (3¾in)

30mm (1¼in)

Fig. 6

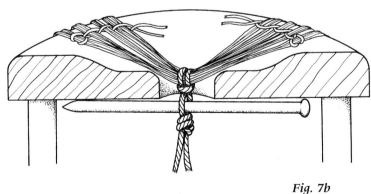

Fig. 7b

Dressing the Maru Dai for Wrapped-loop End

This is suitable only for braids that have one or two ends per bobbin.

Fig. 8a

1 After cutting the warp at post A, remove from the posts and open out, leaving the larkshead knot at post B at the centre of the warp (Fig. 8a).

Fig. 8b

2 Decide on the required length of the loop and remove the larkshead knot, wrap the warp and fasten off (Figs. 8b and 8c).

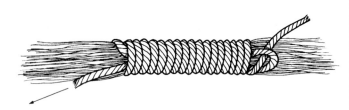

Pull this end until loop is hidden   *Fig. 8c*

Fig. 8d

3 Fold the wrapping to form a loop and interlace left- and right-hand warps, pulling them tightly together (Fig. 8d).

Fig. 8e

4 Tie a loop with thin cotton to hold it in position (Fig 8e).

Fig. 8f

5 Pass the loop down through the centre hole of the Maru Dai and insert the knitting needle, pulling up tight to the underside of the Maru Dai. Remove the thin cotton tie (Fig. 8f).

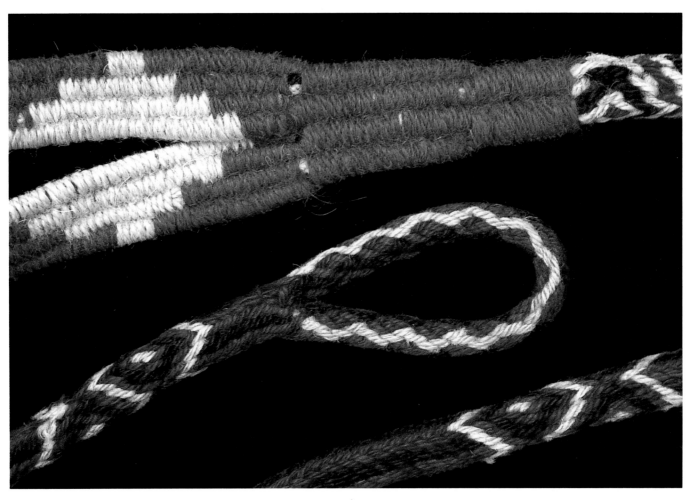

Dressing the Maru Dai for Braided Loop

This is suitable only for braids that have one or two ends per bobbin. The instructions below are for a 16-strand braid.

1 The 16-strand braid is prepared and secured at mid-point with a larkshead knot (Fig. 8a).

2 Decide the required length of the loop to be braided. Tie off the warp tightly at points X and Z, leaving 20mm (⅞in) between them (Fig. 9a).

3 Remove the larkshead knot and feed the tied-off half of the warp down through the centre hole of the Maru Dai. Insert a knitting needle between the two tied-off points and pull the warp up so that the needle touches the underside of the Maru Dai.

A Peruvian sling showing the looped end.

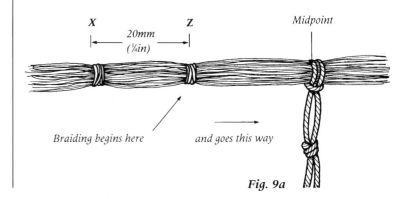

Fig. 9a

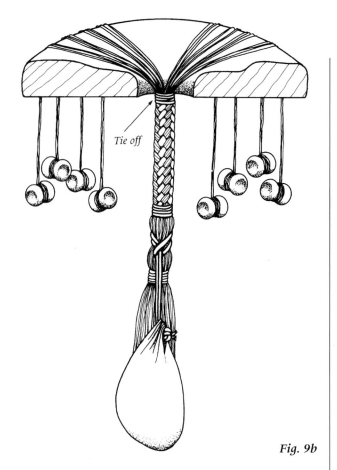

Fig. 9b

4 Wind the warp onto eight bobbins and braid to the required length. Tie off at the end of the braided length (Fig. 9b) and remove the warp from the Maru Dai.
5 Fold the braided warp into a loop and interlace the left- and right-hand threads together. Pull tight and tie with thin cotton to hold their position (Figs. 8d and 8e)
6 Pass the braided loop down through the centre hold of the Maru Dai and secure with a knitting needle (Fig. 8f).

Attaching the Bobbins to the Warp

CONNECTING THE WARP TO THE BOBBIN TIE

This operation, like many others in braiding, has to be completed while the warp is held under tension. It can be kept taut by pulling gently against the Maru Dai.

Making a weaver's knot
1 Slip the loop of the bobbin tie onto the end of the warp, holding the bobbin tie in the left hand and the end of the warp in the right (Fig. 10a).
2 Fold the tail of the warp back over itself, making a loop, and pull the looped tail through the hole that has been made with the left hand (Fig. 10b).
3 Hold the loop in the left hand and pull down tightly onto the bobbin tie (Fig. 10c). The warp is now ready to wind on to the bobbin.

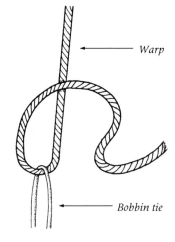

Warp

Bobbin tie

Fig. 10a

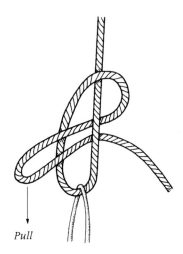

Pull

Fig. 10b

Fig. 10c

Making the Slipping-hitch
This move, which at first
may seem impossible, quickly
becomes second nature.

1 The warp should be
kept taut while it is wound
onto the bobbin. Finish
winding with the warp on
the underside of the bobbin,
400mm (15½in) from the
centre hole of the Maru Dai.

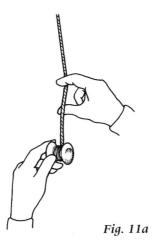

Fig. 11a

2 Hold the bobbin in the
left hand and place the
thumb and finger of the
right hand on the warp
(Fig. 11a).

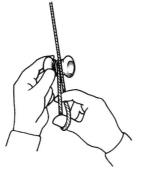

Fig. 11b

3 Swing the bobbin away
from the body, under the
right hand, to form a loop,
using the thumb on the
right hand as an anchor
(Fig. 11b).

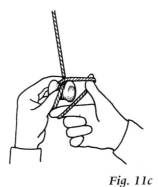

Fig. 11c

4 Flip the right hand
away from the body to the
right to pull the slipping
hitch onto the bobbin,
pulling it tight against the
warp on the bobbin
(Figs. 11c and 11d).

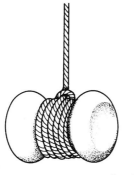

Fig. 11d

SECURING THE COUNTERBALANCE

Calculate the weights required for the counterbalance and
place them in the bag. Fix the bag to the braid on the
underside of the Maru Dai and remove the knitting needle.

Attaching the Bag

Tassel Braids
The bag can be attached in two ways.

1 Make a larkshead knot in the bag tie and secure the bag
on the warp between the two wrapped points (Fig. 12a).
2 Make a loop with a piece of soft cotton and secure the
loop between the two wrapped points with a larkshead
knot. Use a small S-hook to link the loop and the bag
together (Fig. 12b).

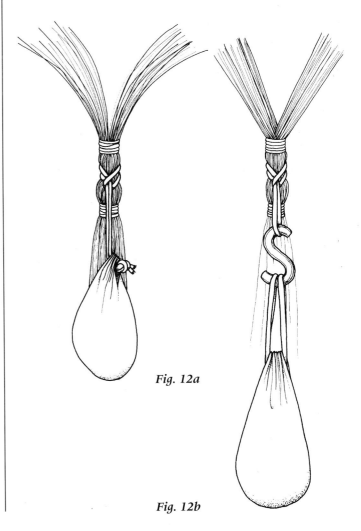

Fig. 12a

Fig. 12b

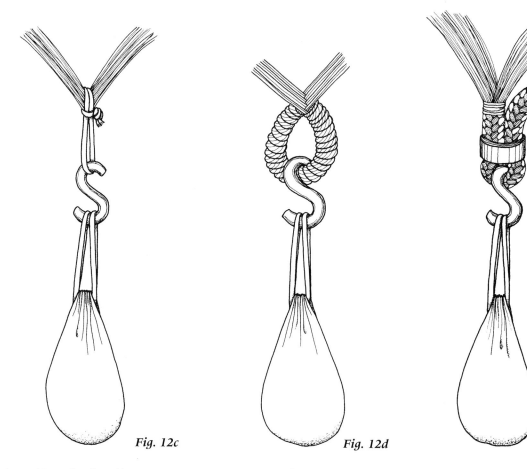

| Fig. 12c | Fig. 12d | Fig. 12e |

Finger-point and Looped-end Braids

When setting up initially, use an S-hook to attach the counterbalance bag to the warp (Figs. 12c and 12d). When the braid is long enough, remove the S-hook and change to the method shown in Fig. 12a or Fig. 12b.

Here is another way of attaching the bag using small rings. It can be used for all braids, except those with a hollow structure.

Collect an assortment of cardboard or wooden tubes of different diameters and from each tube cut a small ring 10mm (⅜in) long. From this selection, a ring can be chosen to suit the thickness of the braid that is being made.

Fold the braid in half and fit a ring over the braid. Insert the S-hook and pull the ring down against the S-hook. Attach the bag to the S-hook (Fig. 12e). Should the braid slip, try a smaller ring, until you find one that grips.

Adjusting the Counterbalance

If you move the counterbalance bag for any reason, it is important to keep the braid under tension and to prevent the bobbins slipping from their last worked position. This is best done by pulling the braid down through the centre hole and inserting a knitting needle through the warp on the underside of the Maru Dai mirror. When this is done, release the braid so that it is pulled up against the needle. This will secure the braid until any adjustment is complete.

This method is also used when you leave a braid unfinished overnight. The knitting needle is inserted and the bag is removed from the braid and rested on the base of the Maru Dai. This prevents the bag tie from making a permanent indentation in the braid.

Adjusting the Bobbins

After the counterbalance has been secured, the bobbins can be arranged around the top of the Maru Dai following the setting-up diagram. When this is done, adjust all the bobbins to the same height.

It is important that all the bobbins are kept at the same height when you are working. Failure to do this will result in an imbalance in tension, which will affect the finish of the braid.

As a guide, the bobbins should be lowered halfway between the underside of the mirror and the base plate. You will find it useful to put a marker on the legs at this height to act as a visual prompt. To lengthen the warp, loosen the slipping-hitch and ease the bobbin down. Then give the bobbin a gentle tug so that the slipping-hitch grips again.

If any bobbins vary in height while you are working, stop and make the necessary adjustments. The bobbins will shorten while working; when they get to a distance of four fingers width from the top of the Maru Dai stop and let them down to the halfway point.

Working at the Maru Dai

SITTING POSITION

Physical characteristics will influence how you sit in front of the Maru Dai, but whatever your individual choice, consider these two measurements (Fig. 13a):

* The top of the Maru Dai should be level with a point on the body that is about midway between the navel and the sternum.
* The distance of the Maru Dai from the body is measured by holding the elbows into the body with the forearms held out at right-angles with the fingers extended. The centre hole of the Maru Dai should be level with the fingertips.

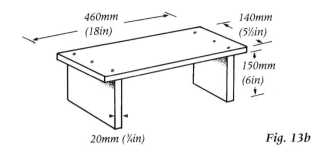

Fig. 13b

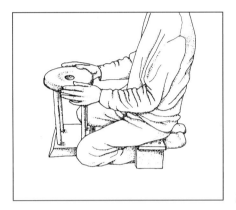

Fig. 13c

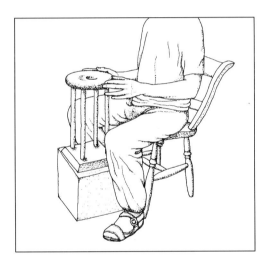

Fig. 13a

A small stool can be a useful aid to sitting comfortably on the floor. It takes the weight of the body without putting pressure on the legs (Figs. 13b and 13c).

Whatever sitting position you choose, your arms, neck and head should remain loose while you work. The body should rock on the hips and not be held stiffly.

The development and practice of these skills will lead to flexible working and the tension will be where it belongs – in the braid and not in the braid-maker.

HAND MOVEMENTS

While you are making braids, most hand movements will be made with both hands working in unison. Many braiders find that they do not move their hands with equal balance – one hand will pull more strongly than the other, and this has the effect of putting a torque in the braid where it is not wanted. A useful way of becoming aware of this imbalance is to learn to juggle. If that is too awe-inspiring, try throwing up and catching two balls or bean bags. Throw them up in the air and observe whether one goes higher. As you practise you will eventually come to understand just how much pressure is required to achieve balanced movement.

BOBBIN MOVEMENTS

The top of the Maru Dai is divided into four compass points. South is nearest the body, north is at the top, east is to the right, and west to the left. Most braids will begin with the bobbins moving from south to north. The example below shows the first step in Design 9.

1 Identify the direction in which the bobbins are to be moved and slide the hands down the warp so that the warp lies across the fingers and the little finger just touches the bobbins (Fig. 14a).

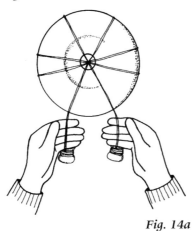

Fig. 14a

2 Lift the bobbins together across the mirror, twisting the wrists inwards so that the palms face down and the warp lies over the thumbs.

3 With the other free fingers, part the warps in the north position and lay the south bobbins in the centre (Fig. 14b).

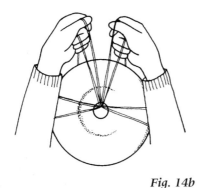

Fig. 14b

4 Bring the north bobbins back to the south position with the warp lying across the fingers (Fig. 14c).

The same movements are used when working from east on the right-hand side to west on the left-hand side.

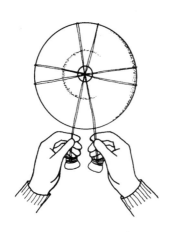

Fig. 14c

Making a Cardboard Maru Dai

BASIC CONSTRUCTION

The plan of the cardboard Maru Dai was designed by Masa Kinoshita, who has given her permission to share her idea in this book. Masa lives in the USA.

This device can be easily made from inexpensive materials and allows the braider to experience the principles of a Maru Dai before going on to buy a wooden one. It can be made from either a thick, solid card or from strong corrugated card. The cutting and assembly instructions are shown below:

1 Cut four side panels
2 × A: 405 × 255mm (16 × 10in)
2 × B: 405 × 255mm (16 × 10in)
Cut out the centre hole in the B panels: 255 × 125mm (10 × 5in) (Fig. 15a). Assemble the four side panels. The two A panels become the sides, and the two B panels are opposite each other, at the front and back. Tape the side panels together, first on the inside to form a box and then on the outside for added strength.

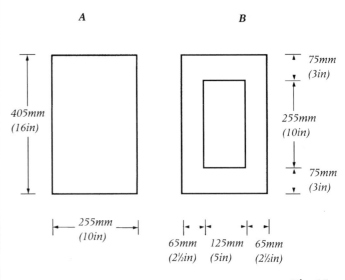

Fig. 15a

Opposite *A cardboard Maru Dai, made from easy-to-find material, allows a beginner to try braiding before buying a wooden stand.*

2 Measure across the base of the assembled side panels to ascertain the size of the base plate. Cut out the square base (Fig. 15b) and tape it to the bottom of the assembled sides. (Our base measured 265mm (10¼in) square using card 2mm (⅛in) thick.)

See step 2   ***Fig. 15b***

3 Cut a circle for the top 405mm (16in) in diameter with a 50mm (2in) diameter hole in the centre (Fig. 15c).

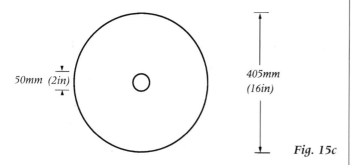

50mm (2in)   *405mm (16in)*

Fig. 15c

4 Position the box upside down on the top and tape the box to the top (Fig. 15d).

The Maru Dai is now complete and ready for use.

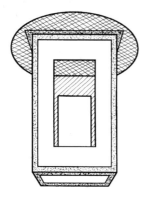

Fig. 15d

BOBBINS

A cheap and simple way to make bobbins is to use empty 35mm film canisters, which are easily obtained from shops that develop photographs. All the canisters should be of equal weight. The fillings can be putty or plasticine, while metal washers or coins are good alternatives. Covering the outside surface of the canister with masking tape will give a good grip for the bobbin tie (Fig. 15e).

Instructions for setting up and braiding are the same as for the wooden Maru Dai.

Fig. 15e

Using the Card Method

Making braids on a card became possible when two pieces of information came together at the same time in 1978. The first was the publication in the United States of a book by Lynn Paulin, *Weaving on Rings and Hoops*, in which a West African braid is shown being made on a square card. The second was the recognition of a connection between the West African braid and the Peruvian sling braid design called Zigzag, shown in D'Harcourt's book *Textiles of Ancient Peru and Their Techniques*. These are, in fact, the same braid. Subsequently, the same pattern was recognized as the Japanese design Maru Genji.

Enquiries made to Lynn Paulin about the card led me to Esther Warner Dendel, who told me that 'these braids were made in West Africa, not on the cards, but with very flexible fingers and toes'. The card device had been introduced into workshops Esther had run in America.

The original connection between the West African and Peruvian braid and the card has been developed over the past 12 years, and it now includes all the sling braiding from Peru, Japanese Kumihimo and the seafaring braids in Ashley's *Book of Knots* (though not all of these are included in this book). A method of notation has been developed for each of the design sections in the book using different sizes of card device.

Opposite *Peruvian sling-makers make all braids by holding the threads in their fists. They make a hole by holding their index finger and thumb together, and the braid grows downwards through the hole. The card method is a mid-way stage between this traditional method and the Maru Dai.*

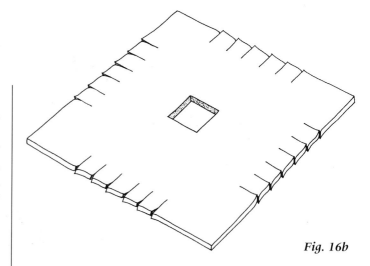

Fig. 16b

MATERIALS FOR THE CARD

Many types of rigid materials have been tested, but cardboard is still found to be the best. It is readily available and, most importantly, holds the threads firmly. There are many kinds of layered display and mounting boards (matt board in the USA) that can be used, but to be effective the card needs to be about 2mm (⅛in) thick. A good alternative is the compressed grey/brown card often found as backing boards to pads of paper available from stationers.

CUTTING AND NUMBERING THE CARD

Six card shapes are needed to make the braids in the design chapters. Details on how to cut and number the card for Designs 1–30 are given below (Fig. 16a); the remaining five card shapes showing numbering and overall measurements follow (Figs. 17a, 17b, 17c, 17d and 17e).

1 Cut a card 130mm (5⅛in) square.
2 Measure and mark the slots and the centre hole.
3 Cut the centre hole with a craft knife to give a clean edge to the hole.
4 Use scissors (not a knife) to cut the slots around the card. The scissor cut should be made deep in the throat of the scissor and not with the points. The cuts made this way hold the threads firmly and tension the braid (Fig. 16b).

5 Take care when cutting the slots around the card. The depth of the cut should be 5–7mm (³⁄₁₆–¼in) – if it is less than 5mm (³⁄₁₆in) the thread may not stay in the slot; if it is greater than 7mm (¼in) the tab between the cuts may bend. The thread should be held in the slot as shown in Fig. 16c. Do not, on any account, cut a V-shape into the slot, because this weakens the card and does not hold the thread well.

6 Number the card, taking care to write the numbers in exactly the same way they are shown in Fig. 16a. Write the letters N, S, E and W around the centre hole; these letters represent the points of the compass and will be explained on page 46.

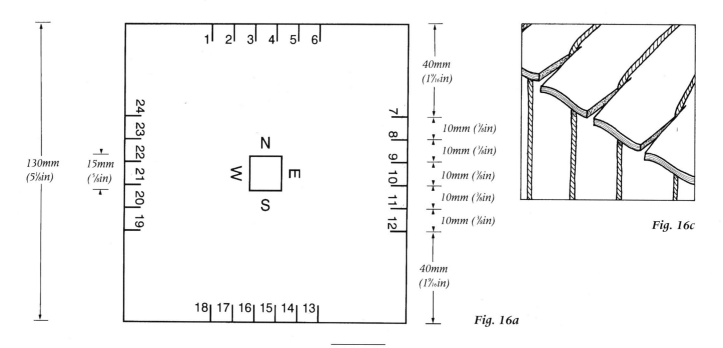

Fig. 16c

Fig. 16a

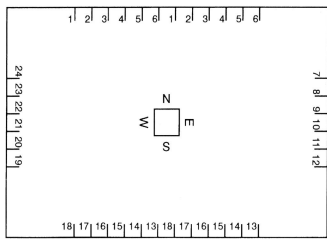

Fig. 17a

Cards for Designs 31–38

Cut a card 190 × 130mm (7½ × 5in) and cut out a 15mm (⅜in) square centre hole. Write the compass points around the hole. Cut and number slots (Fig. 17a), leaving 10mm (⅜in) between slots.

Cards for Designs 39–43

Cut a card 170mm (6⅜in) square and cut out a 15mm (⅜in) square centre hole. Write the compass points around the centre hole. Cut and number slots (Fig. 17b), leaving 10mm (⅜in) between slots.

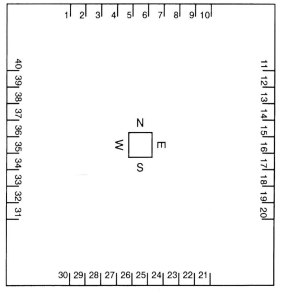

Fig. 17b

Cards for Designs 44–48

Cut a round card 130mm (5in) in diameter and cut out a 15mm (⅜in) square centre hole. Measure and mark 32 slots.

Cut the slots (Fig. 17c) so that they point towards the centre hole. The compass points are not used on this card.

Fig. 17c

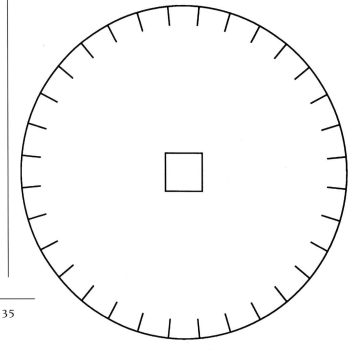

Cards for Designs 49–55

Cut a round card 180mm (7in) in diameter and cut out a 15mm (⅝in) square centre hole. Write the compass points around the centre hole. Measure and mark 48 slots. Cut the slots (Fig. 17d) so that they point towards the centre hole. Number the slots 1–48.

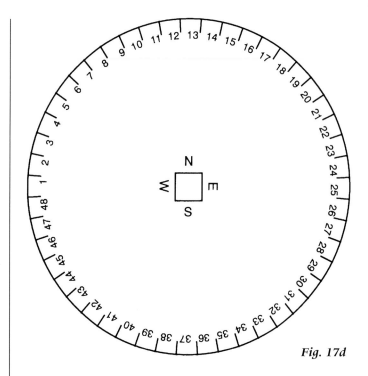

Fig. 17d

Card for Design 56

Cut a round card 230mm (9in) in diameter and cut out a 15mm (⅝in) square centre hole. Measure and mark 80 slots. Cut the slots (Fig. 17e) so that they point towards the centre hole. Number the slots 1–80. The compass points are not used on this card.

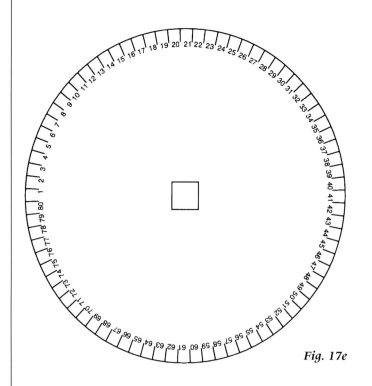

Fig. 17e

BOBBINS

Bobbins are used with the card method to keep the warp ordered and stored. They are not intended to hold the threads under tension, because the slots in the card do this.

The simplest bobbin is made from cardboard (Fig. 18a). The warp is wound around the card and caught in a slot to hold it in place (Figs. 18b and 18c), or a slipping-hitch can be used, instead of a slot, to hold the warp in the same way as for the Maru Dai bobbin.

The warp can be lengthened by unwinding the bobbin and refixing in the slot.

Fig. 18d

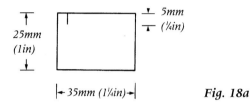

Fig. 18a

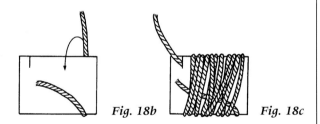

Fig. 18b   Fig. 18c

COUNTERBALANCE

The warps can be held on the underside of the card in one hand while the other hand moves the threads on the top surface. If you prefer, a counterbalance can be attached to the warp under the card, leaving both hands free – a fishing weight of 170gm gives a good tension. The weight is fixed to the warp with a short loop of thread, as for the Maru Dai (Fig. 18e).

THREADING THE WARP

The warps are prepared in exactly the same way as for the Maru Dai. The card method works best with single threads or, at most, with two to three threads per slot.

The prepared warp is inserted through the centre hole and held in place beneath the card with one hand, tight up to the underside of the card. Use the other hand to spread the warp threads over the surface of the card and insert them with a little tension into the slots according to the setting-up diagram.

The warps are wound onto the bobbins so that they all hang down around the card at the same height (Fig. 18d).

Fig. 18e

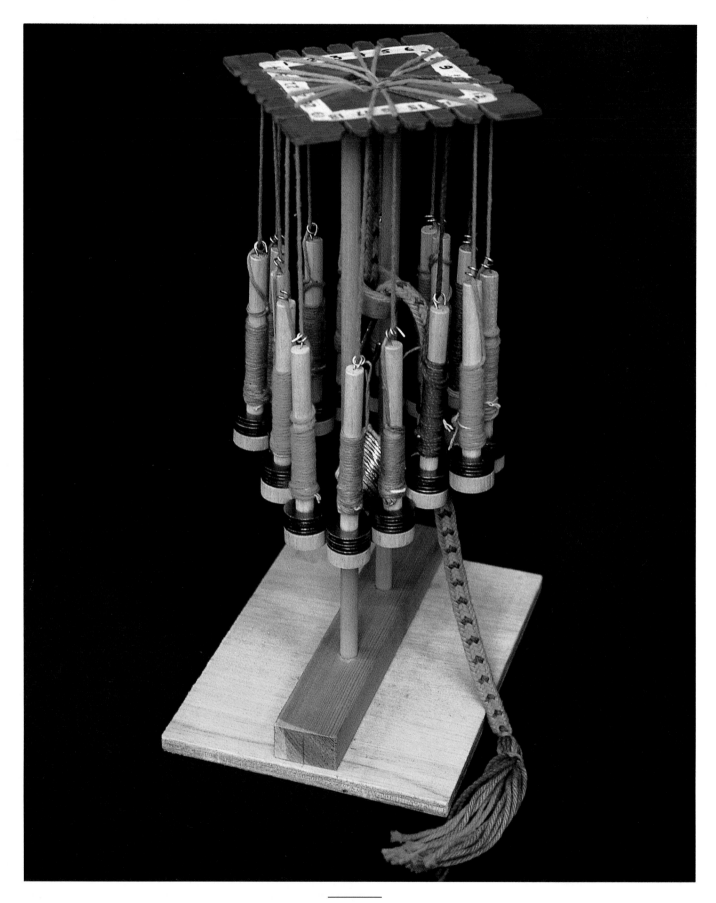

Using the Slotted-board Method

The slotted-board method is an intermediate stage between the card method and the Maru Dai. The braids are made following the card instructions.

The stand shown in Fig. 19a is a support for the slotted board. The board rests unattached on the top of the stand and is kept in place by the bobbin and counterbalance weight. To make the stand prepare the following:

1 plywood base plate 195 × 150 × 8mm (7½ × 6 × ⅜in)
1 softwood dowel support 195 × 30 × 20mm (7½ × 1¼ × ¾in)
2 dowel stand legs 300 × 10mm (12 × ⅜in)
1 plywood top plate 75 × 75 × 2mm (2¾ × 2¾ × ⅛in)

1 Drill two 10mm (⅜in) holes in the dowel support at 65mm (2½in) centres. Glue it to the base plate.
2 Glue the dowel sticks to the dowel support.
3 Screw the top plate to the dowels.

The slotted board shown is for Designs 1–30. It is made from 2mm (⅛in) hardboard to the measurements shown in Fig. 19b. Slotted boards for other designs can be made based on the card measurements; see Figs. 17a–17c.

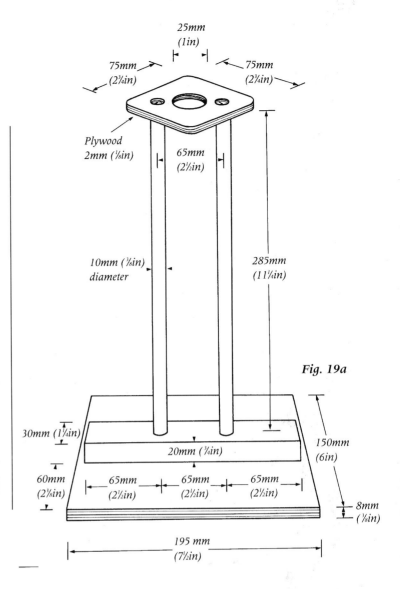

Plywood 2mm (⅛in)

25mm (1in)

75mm (2¾in)   75mm (2¾in)

65mm (2½in)

10mm (⅜in) diameter

285mm (11¼in)

30mm (1¼in)

20mm (¾in)

150mm (6in)

60mm (2½in)

65mm (2½in)   65mm (2½in)   65mm (2½in)

8mm (⅜in)

195 mm (7½in)

Fig. 19a

Opposite A slotted board, which can be easily made, brings together the card method and the principles of the Maru Dai.

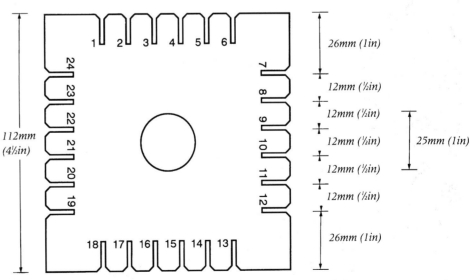

112mm (4½in)

26mm (1in)
12mm (½in)
12mm (½in)
12mm (½in) 25mm (1in)
12mm (½in)
12mm (½in)
26mm (1in)

All slots to be cut 2mm (⅛in) wide by 13mm (½in) deep

Fig. 19b

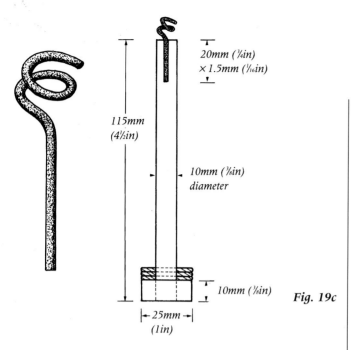

Fig. 19c

The bobbins in Fig. 19c are made from:

1 10mm (⅜in) diameter dowel 115mm (4½in) long
1 1.5mm (¹⁄₁₆in) diameter wire 40mm (1½in) long
1 22mm (⅞in) diameter dowel 10mm (⅜in) long, with a 10mm (⅜in) hole to make the ring.

1   Glue the wooden ring to the dowel.
2   Drill the dowel to take the wire.
3   Form the wire as shown in Fig. 19c and secure in the end of dowel.
4   Thread washers onto the bobbins to the weight required, leaving sufficient room to wind warp onto the bobbin.

The bobbin tie and the warp are both secured in the same way as for the Maru Dai. The warp thread passes through the wire loop to keep the bobbins evenly suspended (Fig. 19d).

Fig. 19d

Finishing and Embellishing

The finishing and embellishing techniques that follow have been selected as illustrations. More elaborate finishes can be employed – for example, attaching tassels made around wooden formers or using beads and gold work. The finishing methods shown can be used at both ends of the braid.

REMOVING A BRAID FROM THE MARU DAI OR CARD

1   Slip the counterbalance bag down the braid so that it rests on the base plate. Pull the braid down and insert a knitting needle through the warp on the underside of the Maru Dai.
2   Tie off the braid with thin cotton threads at a point where the braiding stops to prevent the braid unravelling.
3   Working from south to north, then from east to west, remove the bobbins one at a time. When all the bobbins are removed, slip the counterbalance from the braid.

SIMPLE TASSEL

The ends of the braid can be finished with a simple tassel.

1   Cut a length of thread from one of the colours used to make the braid and thread it onto a needle.
2   Ease the cotton tie onto the loose ends and sew through the braid at an angle (Fig. 20a).

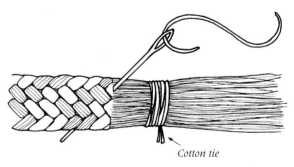

Cotton tie

Fig. 20a

3 Working towards the tassel, wrap the braid firmly, finishing off with an overhand knot (Fig. 20b).

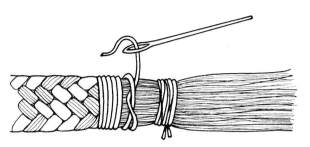

Fig. 20b

4 Stitch over the wrapping three times on both sides of the braid to secure it to the wrapping, and remove the cotton tie (Fig. 20c).

Fig. 20c

When the wrapping is complete, trim the tassel using cellophane or airmail paper. Cut a small piece of cellophane and wrap it around the braid (Fig. 20d). Slide the cellophane down the braid onto the tassel. Determine the tassel length and cut through the cellophane with sharp scissors (Fig. 20e). This helps to keep the ends at one length.

Fig. 20d

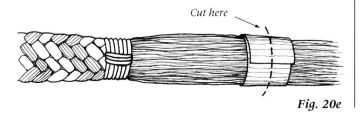

Cut here

Fig. 20e

TASSEL WITH FERRULE

Tie off the braid with a cotton tie as for a simple tassel. Select and cut a ferrule, which should be slightly bigger than the diameter of the braid. Ferrules can be made from wooden beads, perspex, cardboard tube or any material suitable for the effect required.

1 Select one of the yarns used to make the braid and closely wrap the ferrule (Fig. 21a).

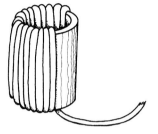

Fig. 21a

2 Slip the wrapped ferrule onto the braid (Fig. 21b). Using a needle, thread the loose warp ends from the tassel back over the ferrule and down between the ferrule and the braid. Pull tight. Repeat until the ferrule is covered with a second layer of threads (Fig. 21c).

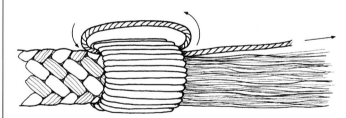

Fig. 21b

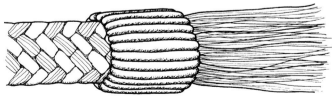

Fig. 21c

To finish the tassel, hold the ferrule in place and trim the loose ends, cutting through the cellophane, as described above (see Fig. 20e).

EMBELLISHING TASSEL ENDS

Several looped and stitched structures can be used to embellish the ends of braids. One of the simplest is buttonhole stitch, which is shown below.

1 Finish off as for a simple tassel (see Figs. 20a–20d).
2 Cut off the tassel close to the wrapping with a sharp scalpel. Apply a clear, all-purpose adhesive to the cut ends (Fig. 22a).

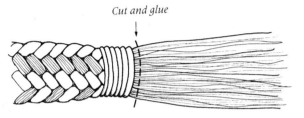

Cut and glue

Fig. 22a

3 Thread a needle and sew through the braid to a point above the wrapping where the buttonholing is to begin. Sew the buttonhole loops, stitching into the the braid for the first row. Then stitch into the loops, moving around the braid and working down towards the cut end (Figs. 22b and 22c). Complete by drawing the loops together over the end of the braid. Secure the loose end by sewing back up through the braid.

Fig. 22b

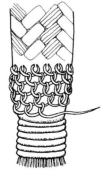

Fig. 22c

SPLIT LOOPS

A split loop can be made at any point along the length of the braid. It involves dividing the braid in two, working with the first group of threads for a certain length and then with the second group, rejoining all the ends together again and continuing the original braid (Fig. 23).

Fig. 23

These brightly coloured wrappings are known as Bolivian tassels, and they are found on braids worn by women to decorate their plaited hair.

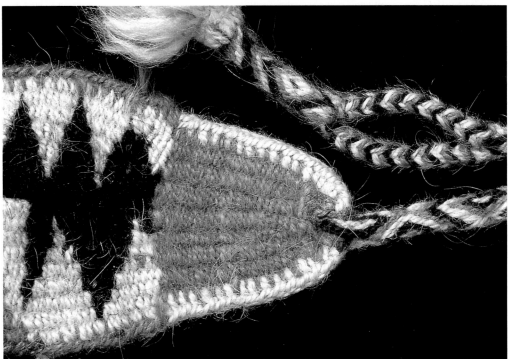

A Peruvian sling with a split loop. Loops can be added to braids anywhere along their length.

BOLIVIAN POMPONS

Bolivian pompons are usually arranged close together in a sequence of graded colours. The method shown here is an interpretation of the technique, rather than the traditional way.

Decide how many colours you wish to use, select one and thread a needle with sufficient yarn to make several pompons.

1 Wrap the thread several times around the braid, to create a foundation to stitch over (Fig 24a).
2 Sew in a circular movement over the wrapping, keeping the stitches 'full' and close together (Fig. 24b).

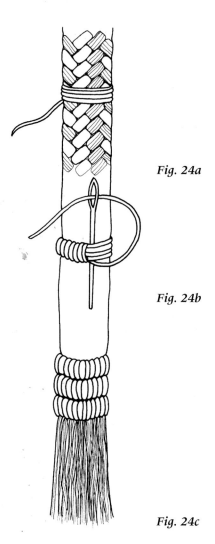

Fig. 24a

Fig. 24b

Fig. 24c

3 Stitch into the braid to finish off, letting the long tail hang down the side of the braid, for later use.

Add pompons, laying them close together (Fig. 24c) until all the colours have been used. Further pompons can be added by picking up and using the long tails.

PERUVIAN TASSELS

These tassels are made during the braiding process by laying cut lengths of yarn across the warp and trapping them into the structure.

1 Cut several lengths of yarn and lay them across the braid structure, east to west. Make south to north moves to trap the cut ends (Fig. 25a).

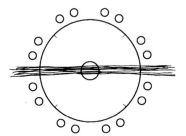

Fig. 25a

2 Place further cut ends across south to north and make east to west moves (Fig. 25b).

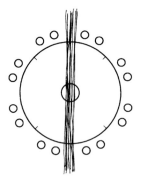

Fig. 25b

3 Continue to make the braid until the next tassel is required, then repeat steps 1 and 2 above.
4 When the braid is complete, smooth the loose ends of each tassel down against the braid, wrap the waist with several turns and secure and trim the length (Fig. 25c).

The head and waist of the tassel can be embellished with embroidered patterns.

Peruvian sling-makers often finish off their dance braids with tassels.

STEAMING AND SHAPING

If you look closely at the finished braid you will see that indentations have been made by the counterweight bag and that the braid may not be exactly straight or round. Steaming the complete length of braid will relax the fibres and will usually correct these faults. Steam the braid by holding it over a jet of steam, being careful not to burn your fingers. A kettle with a spout makes an excellent steamer.

Flat braids can also be shaped by 'flattening' with a rolling pin. Round braids can be rolled 'round' with a flat piece of wood.

Fig. 25c

Introduction to the Design Sections

In the sections that follow there are instructions on how to make a braid using either a Maru Dai or a card. The instructions for both follow the same format for all the designs.

The information shown for each design is described below.

SOURCE

The country shown as the design source should be taken as a guideline only, for braids from different countries often share a common structure. In his book *Interlacing* Jack Lenor Larsen shows a system of analysing structure, which gives an objective approach to the study of braids.

PHOTOGRAPHED SAMPLES

Beneath this heading you will find details of the weights of the bobbins, the counterbalance used and the type of thread. The visual translations of the samples are seen in the colour illustrations at the beginning of each design.

SETTING UP

The setting-up diagrams show where to position the threads around the Maru Dai and card. Letters are used to identify the different colours. Designs 1–43 show colours arranged around squares; these relate to the 'four directions' for the Maru Dai and to the square and rectangular cards. Designs 44–56 use circles, relating to the Maru Dai and the round cards.

WORKING METHOD

This shows the sequence of steps to make the braid. Separate instructions are given for the Maru Dai and the card method.

Maru Dai Instructions

The top surface of the Maru Dai is represented by a large circle and the bobbins by the smaller circles. The bobbins are shown in their working positions. The example in Fig. 26 shows the bobbins arranged for Design 4, step 1. The top surface of the Maru Dai is divided into four areas, which are indicated on each Maru Dai diagram by four small lines on the inside of the large circles. As mentioned before, the area at the top of the circle is north, and south always faces the body. The division of the areas by compass points helps to order the bobbins in their 'home' areas and provides a systematic way of describing the movement of the bobbins.

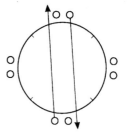

Fig. 26

Moving the Bobbins

Arrows are used to indicate which bobbins are to be moved and where they are to be placed. When it is important to move bobbins in a certain order the bobbins are marked with the numbers 1 and 2, indicating the order in which they are to be moved.

In certain designs it is also necessary to know which hand picks up the bobbins. The letters R or RH are used for right hand and L or LH for left hand.

The example in Fig. 27 from Design 11, step 1 shows both numbers and hand movements.

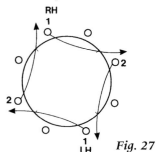

Fig. 27

Card Instructions

Details of how to prepare the cards are shown in Figs. 16 and 17.

Home Slots

Home slots are the slots into which the threads are placed when a card is set up and the slots to which all strands return after completing the moves for each step. The home slots are shown as a sequence of numbers – for example, 3 4   9 10   15 16   21 22.

Two methods of notation are necessary to show the sequence of moves on the card. The first is 'Threads change place'; the second is 'Move'. These are explained below.

Threads Change Place

This means that two threads swap places with each other, either moving in a clockwise or an anticlockwise direction. (see Fig. 28 from Design 1, step 1).

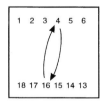

Fig. 28

Move

This instruction is shown as a list of numbers that indicate the sequence in which the threads are to be moved – for example, 4 → 14 means that the thread in slot 4 moves to slot 14. When a sequence of steps has been completed, all the threads will have returned to the home slots. The diagram next to the number sequence shows the 'pathway' the threads will have followed at the completion of the full sequence of steps (see Fig. 29 from Design 4, step 1).

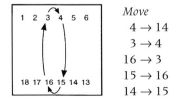

Move

4 → 14
3 → 4
16 → 3
15 → 16
14 → 15

Fig. 29

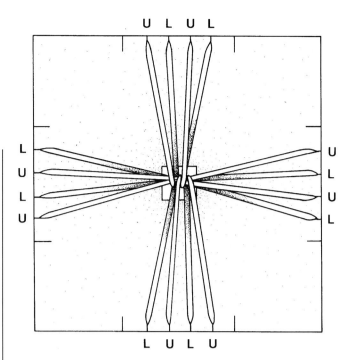

Fig. 30

Repositioning of Threads

The nature of the card method, which involves fixed slots, means that additional moves may have to be included in the sequence of moves, simply to reposition the threads in their home slots or to make a slot available to receive a thread. This usually involves a move to an adjacent slot. In Fig. 29 4 → 14 places a thread to one side so that the pathway moves may commence; 14 → 15 returns the thread to its home slot at the end of the sequence. The repositioning moves are also found as a group of moves at the end of a sequence, under the heading Reposition.

Four Directions – Card Method

Four directions will have been marked on the card. They show the compass points in exactly the same way as the Maru Dai. However, while the Maru Dai remains in a fixed position with the south side facing the body, the card is used in two positions. The south side is held to the body when working the threads south to north. The west side is held to the body when working the threads west to east.

LOWERS AND UPPERS

It is important to know that the threads that are moved in braid-making are called lowers and that the threads that are waiting their turn to move are called uppers.

If you examine the braid you are making you will see that, as it moves, the lower thread forms the stitch on the patterned surface of the braid. Fig. 30 shows Design 26 and the position of the lower and upper threads. Designs 26 and 48 both make spiral patterns, which can be reversed by changing the position of the lowers and uppers.

4- and 8-strand Braids

The section begins with two 4-strand braids, Designs 1 and 2. The roots of these braids lie way back in history, and they would probably have been used to make containers and straps. They are the foundation braids from which many of the braids in this book have developed.

As a result of exploring alternative ways in which to exchange A and B threads, one particular braid-maker developed a third 4-strand braid (Design 3) in 1989, showing us that there are still more structures awaiting discovery by those with a curious mind.

The round and square 8-strand braids, Designs 4–8, are made with various combinations of the clockwise and anti-clockwise movements that derive from the basic 4-strand braid (Design 1). These basic moves will again be seen in the 16- and 24-strand braid structures. Designs 10 and 11 are braids with a hollow structure, and their appearance can be changed dramatically by using thick and thin threads. The moves that make this braid are the same as in maypole dancing, when dancers skip around a circle, weaving in out of their partners to make an interlaced structure around the pole. Maypole dancing is usually done with 12 or 24 ribbons, as can this braid. Later in this book instructions are given for a 16-strand hollow braid (Design 49), and instructions showing how to carry a permanent core inside hollow braids follow Design 11.

Designs 5 and 13 show braids that were discovered by students while attempting to make other designs. If you invent a new design through a happy accident while working, remember to record the moves while you still remember them.

Design 9 is a simple 8-strand braid, which must be attributed to a worldwide source, for the structure is known in many cultures. This design will be seen in many museums, along with other simple braids. It is worth keeping notes of what you see in such collections, for it builds up an understanding of the different braid applications and their origins.

Designs 12–16 are flat braids, which are useful for trimmings, such as edging lampshades, chair seats, cushions and garments.

Opposite *This green and blue necklace was made from Design 4 with spaced-dyed Japanese silk.*

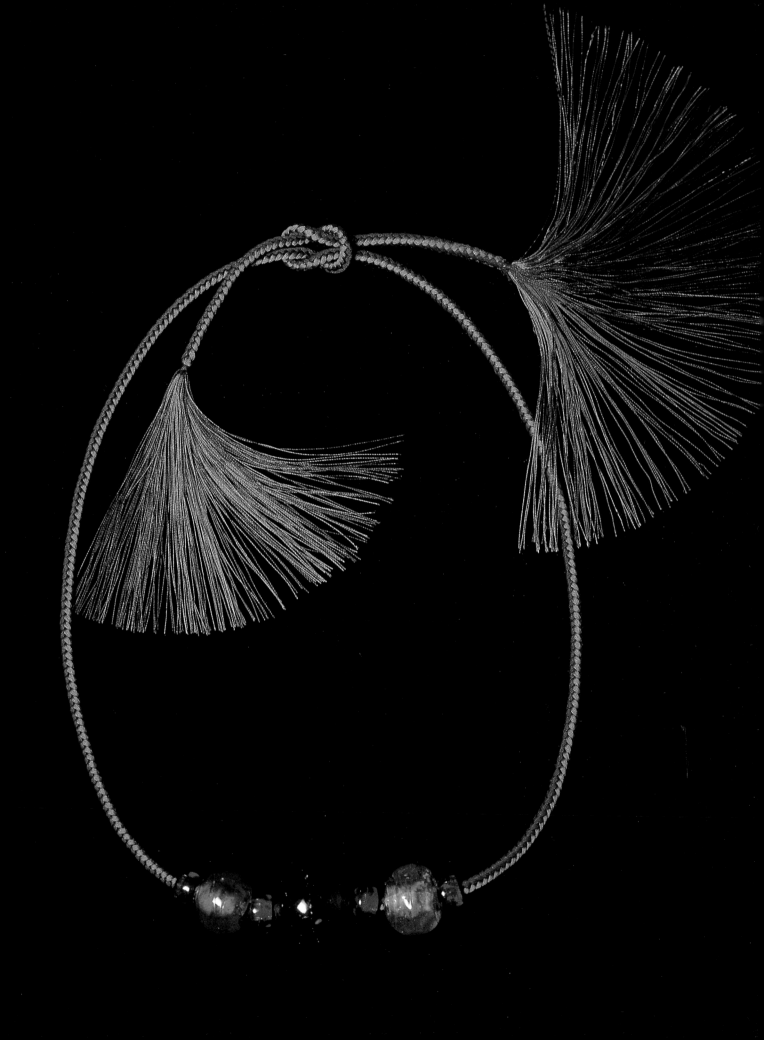

4-strand Round Braid with Two Variations

SETTING UP

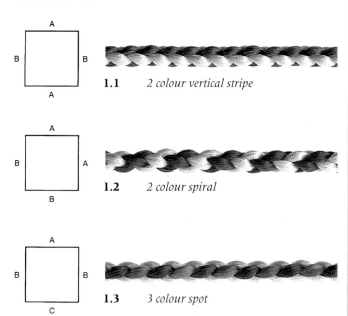

1.1   *2 colour vertical stripe*

1.2   *2 colour spiral*

1.3   *3 colour spot*

PHOTOGRAPHED SAMPLES

These were made using: 70gm bobbins / 160gm counter-balance / 80 ends 150/3 rayon.

WORKING METHOD

To make, continuously repeat steps 1 and 2.

MARU DAI

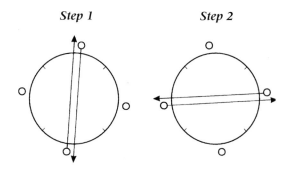

Step 1   *Step 2*

CARD

Home slots   4 9   16 21

Step 1

Step 2

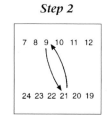

Threads change place   *Threads change place*

4-strand Flat Braid

SETTING UP

AA

BB

2 colour chevron

PHOTOGRAPHED SAMPLE

This was made using: 70gm bobbins / 160gm counter-balance / 80 ends 150/3 rayon.

WORKING METHOD

MARU DAI

To make by Maru Dai, continuously repeat steps 1 and 2.

    Because the structure of this braid is made by south-north moves only, the weight of the bobbins will pull down to the south side of the Maru Dai. Work the braid, allowing it to rest on the south side of the centre hole.

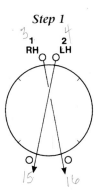

Step 1

1   2
RH   LH

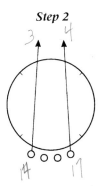

Step 2

CARD

To make by card, continuously repeat steps 1 and 2.

Home slots   3 4   14 17

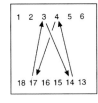

Step 1

1 2 3 4 5 6

18 17 16 15 14 13

Pathway

Move

4 → 16
3 → 15
14 → 4
17 → 3
15 → 14
16 → 17

3

UK

4-strand Flat Braid

SETTING UP

2 colour

PHOTOGRAPHED SAMPLE

This was made using: 70gm bobbins / 160gm counter-balance / 80 ends 150/3 rayon.

WORKING METHOD

To make, continuously repeat steps 1–6.

MARU DAI

Step 1 *Step 2*

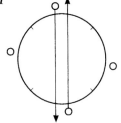
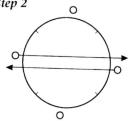

Step 3 *Step 4*

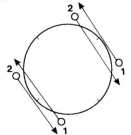
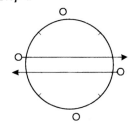

Step 5 *Step 6*

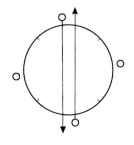
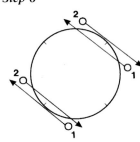

CARD

Home slots   4 9   16 21

Step 1 *Step 2*

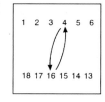
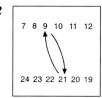

Threads change place   *Threads change place*

Step 3 *Step 4*

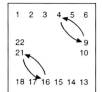
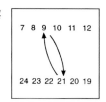

Threads change place   *Threads change place*

Step 5 *Step 6*

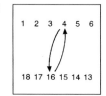
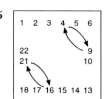

Threads change place   *Threads change place*

8-strand Square Braid · *Vertical Stripe with Two Variations*

SETTING UP

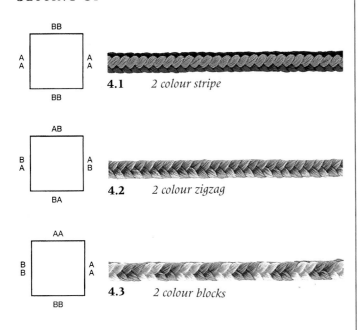

4.1 *2 colour stripe*

4.2 *2 colour zigzag*

4.3 *2 colour blocks*

PHOTOGRAPHED SAMPLES

These were made using: 70gm bobbins / 270gm counter-balance / 40 ends 150/3 rayon.

WORKING METHOD

This braid is derived from Design 1, the basic 4-strand braid. Step 1 is made in a clockwise direction, while step 2 moves anticlockwise. When these two steps are further developed they become the 16-strand braid in Design 17.

To make, continuously repeat steps 1 and 2.

MARU DAI

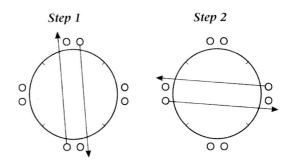

Step 1   *Step 2*

CARD

Home slots   3 4   9 10   15 16   21 22

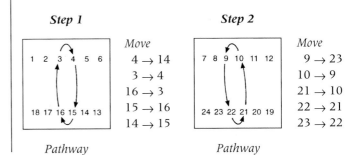

Step 1	*Move*
	4 → 14
	3 → 4
	16 → 3
	15 → 16
	14 → 15

Pathway

Step 2	*Move*
	9 → 23
	10 → 9
	21 → 10
	22 → 21
	23 → 22

Pathway

8-strand Chevron Braid

SETTING UP

2 colour

PHOTOGRAPHED SAMPLE

This was made using: 70gm bobbins / 270gm counter-balance / 40 ends 150/3 rayon.

WORKING METHOD

This pattern is also derived from Design 1. With each step two threads change place with each other, travelling in either a clockwise or an anticlockwise direction. The development of this braid will be found in Design 18, the 16-strand chevron braid.

To make, continuously repeat steps 1 and 2.

MARU DAI

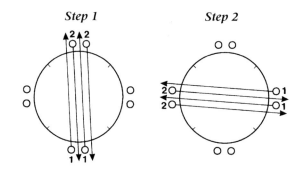

Step 1   *Step 2*

CARD

Home slots   3 4   9 10   15 16   21 22

Step 1

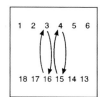

Threads change place

Step 2

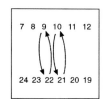

Threads change place

8-strand Round Braid with Linked Diamonds

SETTING UP

2 colour

PHOTOGRAPHED SAMPLE

This was made using: 70gm bobbins / 360gm counter-balance / 40 ends 150/3 rayon.

WORKING METHOD

In steps 1 and 2 the threads move in a clockwise direction; in steps 3 and 4 the threads move in an anticlockwise direction.

To make, continuously repeat steps 1–4.

MARU DAI

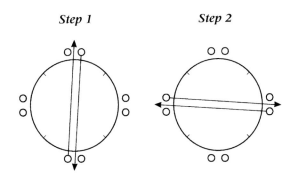

Step 1   *Step 2*

Step 3   *Step 4*

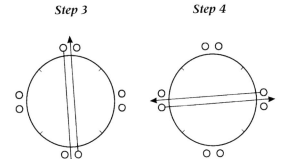

CARD

Home slots   3 4   9 10   15 16   21 22

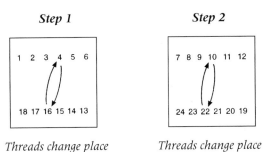

Step 1   *Step 2*

Threads change place   *Threads change place*

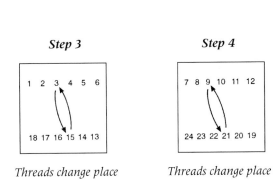

Step 3   *Step 4*

Threads change place   *Threads change place*

8-strand Braid · *Diamond with Four Variations*

SETTING UP

7.1 *2 colour*

7.2 *3 colour*

7.3 *3 colour*

7.4 *3 colour*

7.5 *4 colour*

PHOTOGRAPHED SAMPLES

These were made using: 70gm bobbins / 360gm counter-balance / 40 ends 150/3 rayon.

WORKING METHOD

The diamond patterns are made up of four threads that zigzag down the length of the braid, enclosing the other four threads that form the diamond centre. In pattern 7.1 the A threads are the outlining threads and the B threads form the centre of the diamond.

The five patterns can be made with threads all the same thickness, or texture can be added by increasing the thickness of the B threads.

When working on the Maru Dai, a better defined outline can be made by slightly lifting the bobbins upwards as they cross and pass each other over the top of the Maru Dai. A braid with a flatter appearance can be made by reducing the counterbalance weight to about 25 per cent of the total bobbin weight.

This design combines the moves from Designs 4 and 5, and the development of this braid will be found in Design 19, the 16-strand diamond design.

To make, continuously repeat steps 1–8.

MARU DAI

Step 1
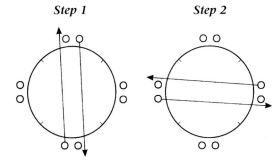

Step 2

Step 3
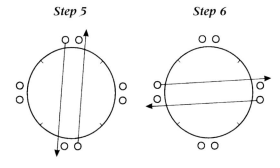

Step 4

Step 5
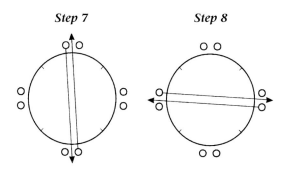

Step 6

Step 7

Step 8

CARD

Home slots   3 4   8 10   15 16   20 22

Step 1
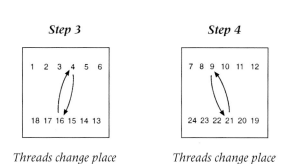

	1 2 3 4 5 6		*Move*
	18 17 16 15 14 13		4 → 14
			3 → 4
			16 → 3
			15 → 16
			14 → 15

Pathway

Step 2

7 8 9 10 11 12	*Move*
24 23 22 21 20 19	9 → 23
	10 → 9
	21 → 10
	22 → 21
	23 → 22

Pathway

Step 3

1 2 3 4 5 6

18 17 16 15 14 13

Threads change place

Step 4

7 8 9 10 11 12

24 23 22 21 20 19

Threads change place

Step 5
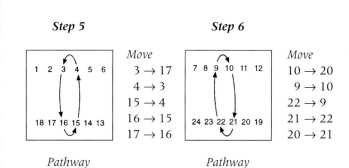

1 2 3 4 5 6	*Move*
18 17 16 15 14 13	3 → 17
	4 → 3
	15 → 4
	16 → 15
	17 → 16

Pathway

Step 6

7 8 9 10 11 12	*Move*
24 23 22 21 20 19	10 → 20
	9 → 10
	22 → 9
	21 → 22
	20 → 21

Pathway

Step 7
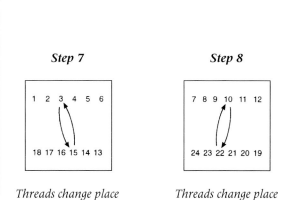

1 2 3 4 5 6

18 17 16 15 14 13

Threads change place

Step 8

7 8 9 10 11 12

24 23 22 21 20 19

Threads change place

8-strand Square Braid · *Vertical Stripe with Three Variations*

SETTING UP

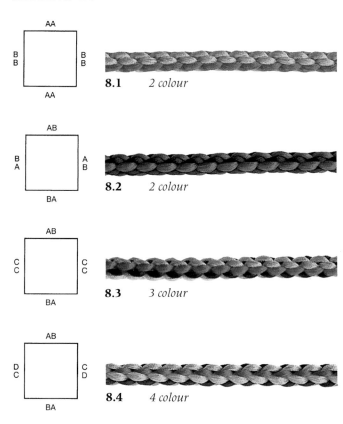

8.1   *2 colour*

8.2   *2 colour*

8.3   *3 colour*

8.4   *4 colour*

PHOTOGRAPHED SAMPLES

These were made using: 70gm bobbins / 270gm counter-balance / 40 ends 150/3 rayon.

WORKING METHOD

In Design 6 two clockwise moves are followed by two anti-clockwise moves. In this design, however, the movements alternate. Steps 1 and 3 are clockwise; steps 2 and 4 turn anticlockwise.

To make, continuously repeat steps 1–4.

MARU DAI

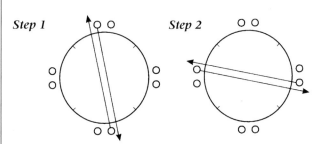

Step 1   *Step 2*

Step 3   *Step 4*

CARD

Home slots   3 4   9 10   15 16   21 22

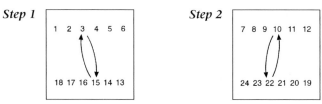

Step 1   *Step 2*

Threads change place   *Threads change place*

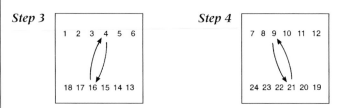

Step 3   *Step 4*

Threads change place   *Threads change place*

8-strand Square Braid · *Vertical Stripe with Two Variations*

SETTING UP

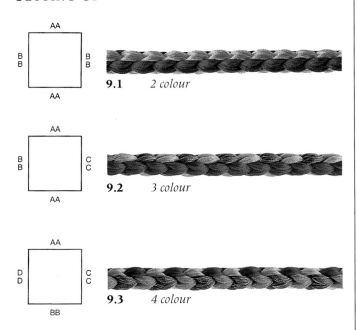

9.1 *2 colour*

9.2 *3 colour*

9.3 *4 colour*

PHOTOGRAPHED SAMPLES

These were made using: 70gm bobbins / 270gm counter-balance / 40 ends 150/3 rayon.

WORKING METHOD

The moves that make this 8-strand braid are the basic moves for the 16-strand braid known in Japan as Maru Genji (see Design 30). The design is also found in Tibet, Peru and West Africa.

To make, continuously repeat steps 1 and 2.

MARU DAI

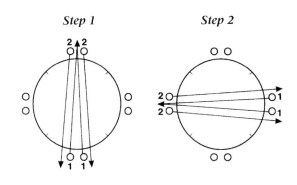

Step 1   *Step 2*

CARD

Home slots   3 4   9 10   15 16   21 22

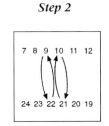

Step 1   *Step 2*

Threads change place   *Threads change place*

8-strand Round Braid · *Vertical Stripe with Five Variations*

SETTING UP

Patterns 10.1, 10.2 and 10.3 can be made by both Maru Dai and card methods using threads of the same thickness.

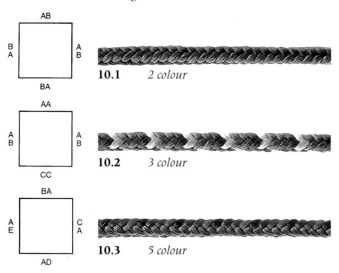

10.1   *2 colour*

10.2   *3 colour*

10.3   *5 colour*

Patterns 10.4, 10.5 and 10.6 are not suitable for the card method. These patterns are made on the Maru Dai with threads of differing thickness, and the threads shown in the north-south position are at least four times the thickness of the east-west threads.

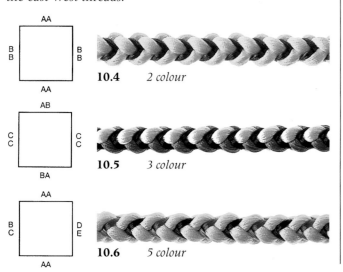

10.4   *2 colour*

10.5   *3 colour*

10.6   *5 colour*

PHOTOGRAPHED SAMPLES

Patterns 10.1, 10.2 and 10.3 were made using: 70gm bobbins / 270gm counterbalance / 40 ends 150/3 rayon.

Patterns 10.4, 10.5 and 10.6 were made using: 100gm bobbins / 380gm counterbalance / 120 ends 150/3 rayon / 28 ends 150/3 rayon.

PREPARING THE MARU DAI FOR PATTERNS 10.4, 10.5 AND 10.6

Wrap towelling around the legs and fasten in position as shown in Fig. 31. The bobbins should rest against the towel without moving.

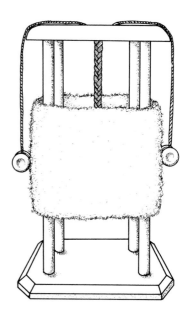

Fig. 31

PREPARING THE THICK THREADS

Arrange the bobbins around the Maru Dai with the large threads in north-south position. Spin the bobbins with the thicker threads in the direction of the arrows (Fig. 32) to give a tight, firm S or Z twist. After twisting the thread, lay the bobbins against the towel, which prevents them from untwisting while you work. Re-twist when necessary during the making process.

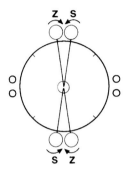

Fig. 32

WORKING METHOD

The following making instructions apply to all six designs.

MARU DAI

To make by Maru Dai, continuously repeat steps 1–4.

Before commencing the braid, re-arrange the north/south bobbins. Cross the north bobbins right over left, and the bobbins in the south position left over right.

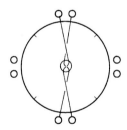

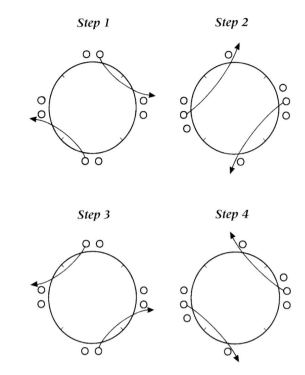

Step 1   *Step 2*

Step 3   *Step 4*

CARD

Home slots   3 4   9 10   15 16   21 22

To make by card, continuously repeat steps 1 and 2.

Before commencing the braid, arrange the threads into their crossed-over positions by moving

4 → 2	16 → 14
3 → 4	15 → 16
2 → 3	14 → 15

then continue with steps 1 and 2.

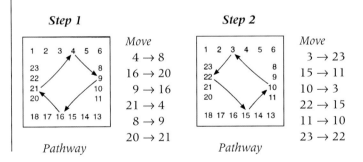

Step 1

Move
4 → 8
16 → 20
9 → 16
21 → 4
8 → 9
20 → 21

Pathway

Step 2

Move
3 → 23
15 → 11
10 → 3
22 → 15
11 → 10
23 → 22

Pathway

8-strand Hollow Braid · *Spiral with 15 Variations*

SETTING UP

Patterns 11.1–11.10 can be made by both Maru Dai and card methods using threads of the same thickness.

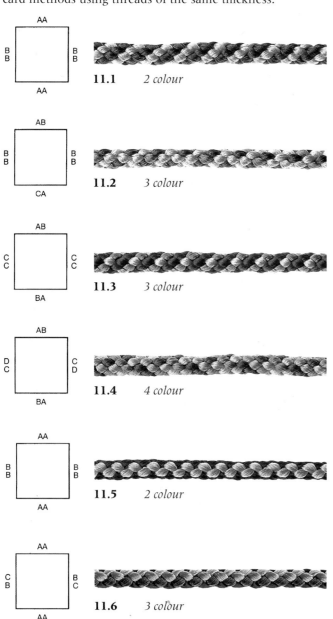

11.1 *2 colour*

11.2 *3 colour*

11.3 *3 colour*

11.4 *4 colour*

11.5 *2 colour*

11.6 *3 colour*

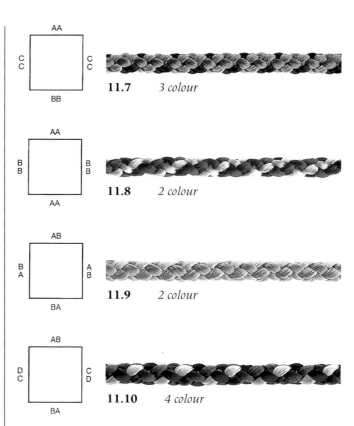

11.7 *3 colour*

11.8 *2 colour*

11.9 *2 colour*

11.10 *4 colour*

Patterns 11.11–11.16 are not suitable for the card method. These are made on the Maru Dai with threads of different thickness. The north-south threads are at least four times the thickness of the east-west threads.

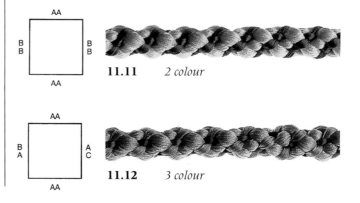

11.11 *2 colour*

11.12 *3 colour*

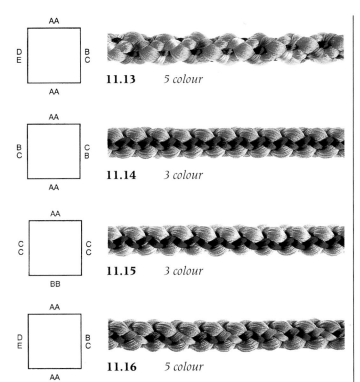

11.13   *5 colour*

11.14   *3 colour*

11.15   *3 colour*

11.16   *5 colour*

PHOTOGRAPHED SAMPLES

Patterns 11.1–11.10 were made using: 70gm bobbins / 280gm counterbalance / 80 ends 150/3 rayon.

Patterns 11.11–11.16 were made using: 100gm bobbins / 380gm counterbalance / 120 ends 150/3 rayon / 28 ends 150/3 rayon.

To make this round, hollow braid, the bobbins travel around the Maru Dai in clockwise and anticlockwise movements. It is these very same movements that are made with ribbons around a maypole, and, like maypole dancing, the braid can be made around a solid core – for example, a dowel, a tube, a piece of wire or a core of other threads (see the notes that follow Design 11 on core-carrying braids). This braid is the foundation structure on which 12-, 16-, 24- and 32-strand hollow braids are made. See Design 49 for a 16-strand hollow braid.

WORKING METHOD

The basic braid is made up of two steps. By extending these two steps two or three times, the structure is changed, resulting in new patterns.

Patterns 11.1–11.16 can all be made on the Maru Dai. Patterns 11.1–11.10 can be made by the card method.

The various setting-up patterns are made by continuously repeating the basic steps in the various sequences shown below:

Pattern	make steps in this sequence
1–4	1 2 repeat
5–7	1 1 2 2 repeat
8–10	1 1 1 2 2 2 repeat
11–13	1 2 repeat
14–16	1 1 2 2 repeat

To make patterns 11.11–11.16 with thick and thin threads, wrap towelling around the legs of the Maru Dai as in Design 10. Spin the thick threads located in the north and south positions with S and Z twists and lay them flat against the towelling (see Fig. 32 in Design 10). Re-twist when necessary during the making process.

MARU DAI

Before you begin to make a braid, space the bobbins equally around the Maru Dai as shown in the diagram in step 1 below.

Make to the sequence of steps shown under Working Method.

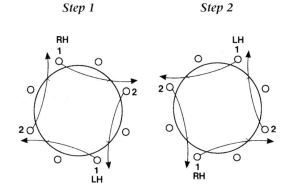

Step 1   *Step 2*

While making, 'drop' the bobbin into the new position. This gives the braid a rounder, tighter finish.

CARD

Home slots   3 4   9 10   15 16   21 22

To make by card, continuously repeat the sequence of steps for the chosen pattern, as shown under Working Method.

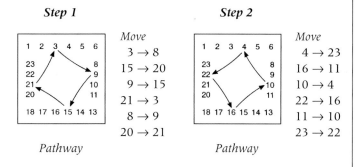

Step 1

1 2 **3** 4 5 6	
23	8
22	9
21	10
20	11
18 17 16 **15** 14 13	

Pathway

Move

3 → 8
15 → 20
9 → 15
21 → 3
8 → 9
20 → 21

Step 2

1 2 **3** 4 5 6	
23	8
22	9
21	10
20	11
18 17 **16** 15 14 13	

Pathway

Move

4 → 23
16 → 11
10 → 4
22 → 16
11 → 10
23 → 22

CORE-CARRYING BRAIDS

Deciding to make a core braid will come as part of the design process – that is, it will arise from a wish to achieve a certain effect. Almost all round and square-sectioned braids can carry a core, and the choice of braid will be influenced by the size, type and ultimate use of the core design.

There are two types of core braid: passive and active. The passive core, because of its nature, always remains in the centre of the braid and does not interchange with the active threads, which move around the passive core. The passive core can made of any material, the nature of the material dictating how the core will be introduced to the braid. The active core has a planned number of threads in the core, which interact with the setting-up threads as part of the overall design. Active core designs are not included in this book.

The core can consist of multiple threads or it can be a single flexible or rigid substance; it can also be temporarily in the braid during the making process.

MULTIPLE ENDS

In this case the core is used as a support and increases the diameter of the braid. The core threads are incorporated in the tassel, but when setting up, the core is separated out and the braid is made around the core.

MARU DAI

For the Maru Dai the core is suspended above the centre hole (Fig. 33).

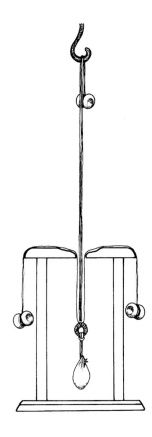

Fig. 33

CARD

For the card method the core is left loosely lying on the card and is flipped from side to side while the active threads are manipulated around the core. The examples in Fig. 34 are taken from the 8-strand braid, Design 11, and show how the passive core is held out of the way while the active threads are moved.

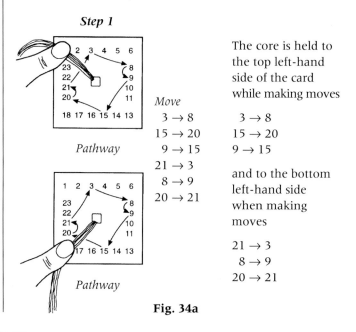

Step 1

Pathway

Pathway

Move

3 → 8
15 → 20
9 → 15
21 → 3
8 → 9
20 → 21

The core is held to the top left-hand side of the card while making moves

3 → 8
15 → 20
9 → 15

and to the bottom left-hand side when making moves

21 → 3
8 → 9
20 → 21

Fig. 34a

Step 2

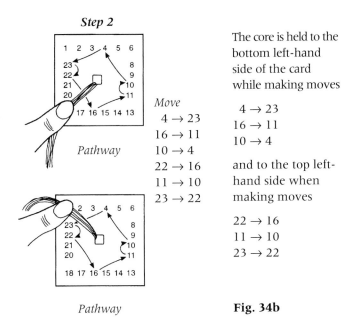

Pathway

Pathway

Move
4 → 23
16 → 11
10 → 4
22 → 16
11 → 10
23 → 22

The core is held to the bottom left-hand side of the card while making moves

4 → 23
16 → 11
10 → 4

and to the top left-hand side when making moves

22 → 16
11 → 10
23 → 22

Fig. 34b

FLEXIBLE CORE

Bendable wire, plastic tube or cord can be used, and these would be supported in a similar way to the multiple cores.

RIGID CORES

Solid cores, such as steel rod, wooden dowel or perspex tubing, will stand freely, but will need a support to keep the core upright. The length and weight of a solid core makes it unsuitable for the card method.

When you are using the Maru Dai, simply remove the base plate and place the Maru Dai over a suitably constructed 'hole' that will take the length of core (Fig. 35).

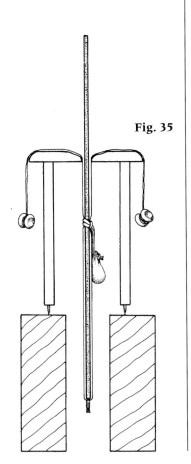

Fig. 35

TEMPORARY CORES

A temporary core is used to create a permanent hollow braid. A wooden dowel 300mm (12in) long with a pointed end is useful for temporary cores. The diameter of the dowel can be varied according to the requirements of the design. When you begin to make the braid around a dowel, keep the dowel in an upright position and attach the bag to the tassel end (Fig. 36). As the braid grows, so the stick will disappear into the braid. When the bag touches the base plate, move the bag to a higher point. Grip and twist the dowel, pulling it clear to a point where it is upright and where sufficient dowel is free to braid around (Fig. 37). Repeat this sequence until the braid is complete.

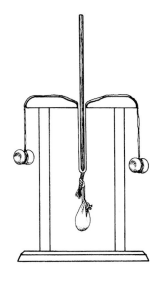

Fig. 36

Fig. 37

8-strand Flat Braid · *Chevron with Two Variations*

SETTING UP

There are two design possibilities with this braid, because the patterns on the front and reverse are different.

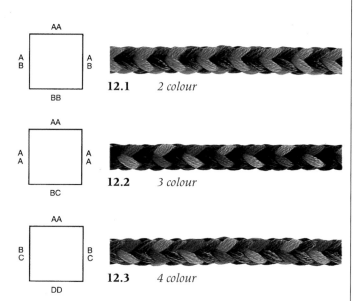

12.1   *2 colour*

12.2   *3 colour*

12.3   *4 colour*

PHOTOGRAPHED SAMPLES

These were made using: 70gm bobbins / 280gm counterbalance / 15 ends 20/2 cotton.

WORKING METHOD

MARU DAI

To make by Maru Dai, continuously repeat steps 1–4.

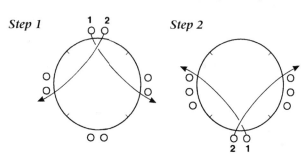

Step 1

Step 2

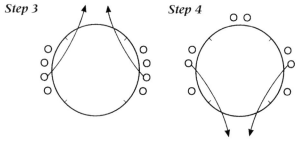

Step 3   *Step 4*

To keep the edges of the braid straight and firm, in steps 3 and 4 bring the bobbins to the centre of the Maru Dai and lift gently before lowering into position.

CARD

Home slots   3 4   9 10   15 16   21 22

To make by card, continuously repeat steps 1 and 2.

Step 1

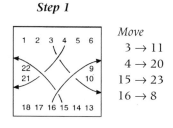

Move
3 → 11
4 → 20
15 → 23
16 → 8

Pathway

Step 2

Move	Reposition
10 → 4	8 → 9
21 → 3	11 → 10
9 → 15	23 → 22
22 → 16	20 → 21

Pathway

8-strand Flat Braid · *Zigzag with Three Variations*

SETTING UP

This design is one of those happy accidents. It was discovered by a student who was attempting Design 12, and it demonstrates how much more there is to discover.

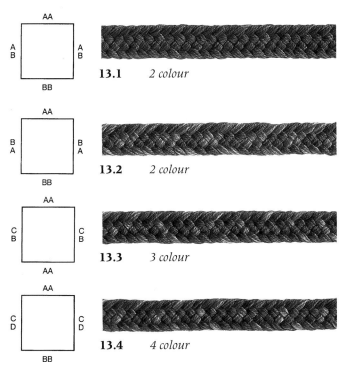

13.1   *2 colour*

13.2   *2 colour*

13.3   *3 colour*

13.4   *4 colour*

PHOTOGRAPHED SAMPLES

These were made using: 70gm bobbins / 280gm counter-balance / 15 ends 20/2 cotton.

WORKING METHOD

MARU DAI

Before making, re-arrange the bobbins in the north position by crossing left over right.

To make by Maru Dai, continuously repeat steps 1–4.

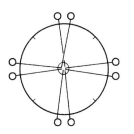

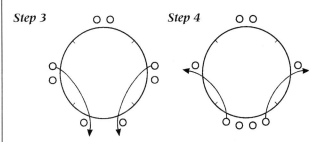

Step 1   **Step 2**

Step 3   **Step 4**

To keep the edges of the braid straight and firm, in steps 3 and 4 bring the bobbins to the centre of the Maru Dai and lift gently before lowering into position.

CARD

Home slots   3 4   9 10   15 16   21 22

Before making, set the threads into their crossed-over position by moving 3 → 5, 4 → 3, 5 → 4.

To make by card, continuously repeat steps 1 and 2.

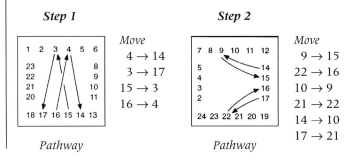

Step 1

Move
4 → 14
3 → 17
15 → 3
16 → 4

Pathway

Step 2

Move
9 → 15
22 → 16
10 → 9
21 → 22
14 → 10
17 → 21

Pathway

8-strand Flat Braid · *Vertical Stripe with Three Variations*

SETTING UP

This braid is oval in section.

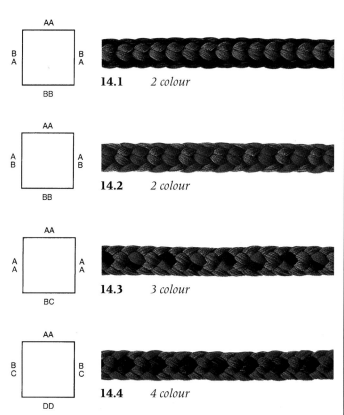

14.1 *2 colour*

14.2 *2 colour*

14.3 *3 colour*

14.4 *4 colour*

PHOTOGRAPHED SAMPLES

These were made using: 70gm bobbins / 280gm counter-balance / 80 ends 200/3 cotton.

WORKING METHOD

MARU DAI

To make by Maru Dai, continuously repeat steps 1–4.

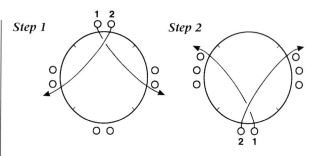

Step 1　　　　*Step 2*

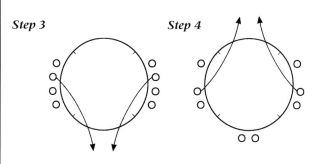

Step 3　　　　*Step 4*

To keep the edges of the braid straight and firm, in steps 3 and 4 bring the bobbins to the centre of the Maru Dai and lift gently before lowering into position.

CARD

Home slots 　3 4　　9 10　　15 16　　21 22

To make by card, continuously repeat steps 1 and 2.

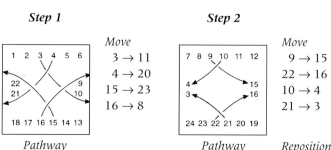

Step 1		*Step 2*	
Pathway	Move	*Pathway*	Move
	3 → 11		9 → 15
	4 → 20		22 → 16
	15 → 23		10 → 4
	16 → 8		21 → 3
			Reposition
			8 → 9
			11 → 10
			23 → 22
			20 → 21

8-strand Flat Braid · *Diagonal Stripe with Two Variations*

SETTING UP

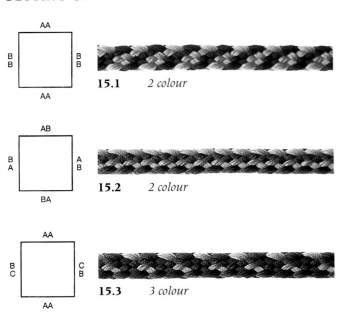

15.1 *2 colour*

15.2 *2 colour*

15.3 *3 colour*

PHOTOGRAPHED SAMPLES

These were made using: 70gm bobbins / 280gm counter-balance / 10 ends 45/3 silk.

WORKING METHOD

MARU DAI

To make by Maru Dai, continuously repeat steps 1–4.

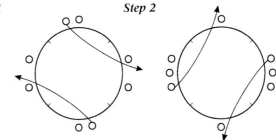

Step 1   *Step 2*

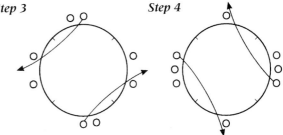

Step 3   *Step 4*

While making, drop the bobbins into position to give a firm, flat braid.

CARD

Home slots   3 4   8 11   15 16   20 23
   To make by card, continuously repeat steps 1 and 2.

Step 1

Pathway

Move
3 → 9
15 → 21
8 → 15
20 → 3

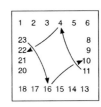

Step 2

Pathway

Move
4 → 22
16 → 10
11 → 4
23 → 16

Reposition
9 → 8
10 → 11
21 → 20
22 → 23

16

JAPAN

8-strand Flat Braid · *Chevron with One Variation*

SETTING UP

ABBA

ABBA

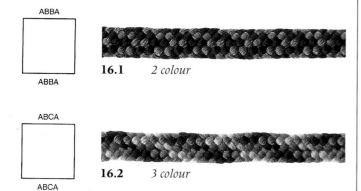

16.1   *2 colour*

ABCA

ABCA

16.2   *3 colour*

PHOTOGRAPHED SAMPLES

These were made using: 70gm bobbins / 280gm counter-balance / 10 ends 35/3 silk.

WORKING METHOD

MARU DAI

To make by Maru Dai, continuously repeat steps 1–3.

Step 1

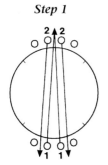

Step 2

Step 3

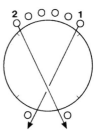

To keep the braid firm use a counterbalance that is 50 per cent of the total bobbin weight. Adjust the tension while working step 3.

CARD

Home slots   1 2 5 6   13 14 17 18

To make by card, continuously repeat steps 1 and 2.

Step 1

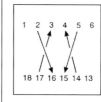

Pathway

Move
14 → 4
17 → 3
5 → 15
2 → 16

Step 2

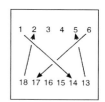

Pathway

Move
13 → 5
18 → 2
16 → 18
15 → 13
6 → 17
1 → 14

Reposition
2 → 1
3 → 2
5 → 6
4 → 5

Opposite   *Design 4, worked in spaced-dyed Japanese silk, was used for this versatile piece, which can be worn as a belt or as a necklace.*

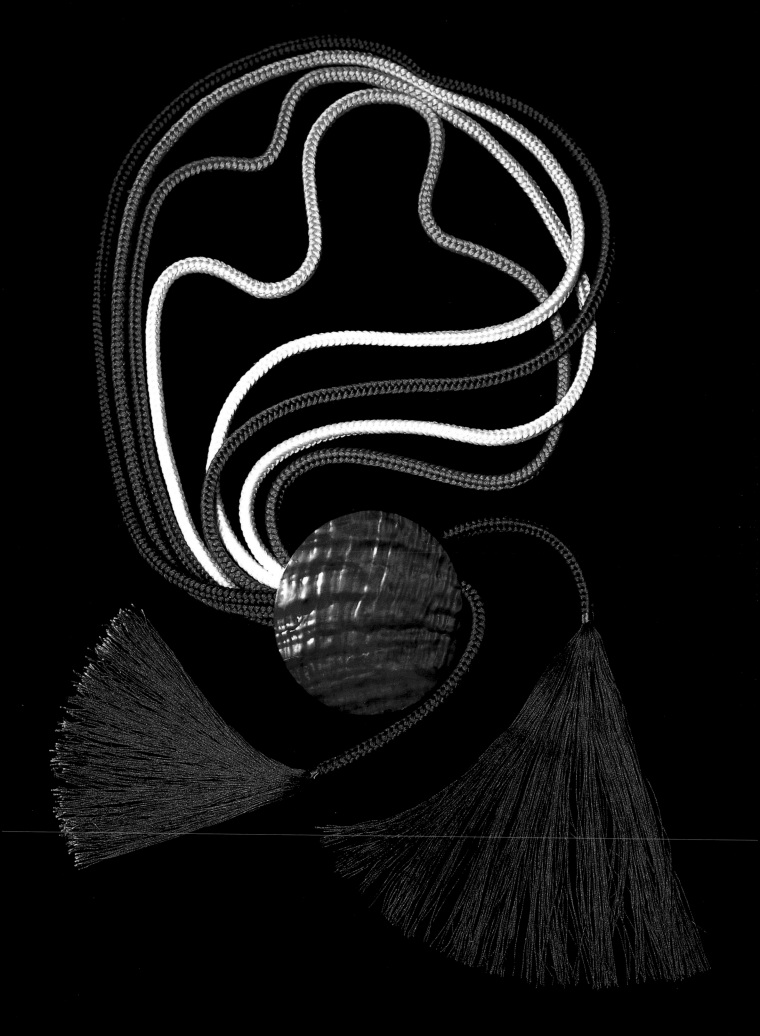

16-strand Braids

Design 17 is made by repeating clockwise and anticlockwise moves. The basic pattern results in a vertical stripe in which the stitches lie to the left or right at an oblique angle. These stitches form the top and bottom of the diamond designs.

Design 18 produces a chevron pattern made with vertical stitches. These stitches form the centre of the diamond designs and are responsible for inverting the structure to change the direction of the stitches.

Designs 19–26 have a common structure and are made by combining the moves of Designs 17 and 18 in a variety of sequences. Designs 27–30 have different structures.

MARU DAI INSTRUCTIONS

The Maru Dai instructions for the braids in this section are given in a step-by-step sequence for each design.

CARD METHOD

There is a good deal of repetition in the moves that make up Designs 17–26, so a system called 'key moves' and 'inversion moves' has been introduced.

The detailed moves are given once only in this introduction, and are then shown in each design by a reference in a small box next to the Maru Dai instructions, rather than a complete set of pathway diagrams and moves for each design.

The reference for each key move uses the first pair of slot numbers that appears at the head of a sequence of moves – for example, 5 → 13, 8 → 24, 2 → 18 and 11 → 19.

Fig. 38 shows an example, taken from Design 19, step 1, of how a key move is represented. The reference for each inversion move uses the slot numbers of the two pairs of threads that change place.

Fig. 39 shows an example, taken from Design 19, step 3, of how an inversion move is represented.

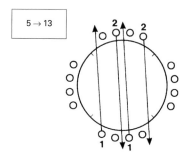

Fig. 38

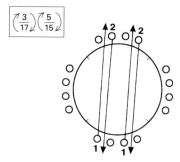

Fig. 39

CARD METHOD KEY AND INVERSION MOVES

You might find it helpful to photocopy this page so that you can keep it to hand for easy reference while working on Designs 17–26, Design 31 and Design 37.

KEY MOVES

The key moves are shown at the head of the four columns – that is, 5 → 13, 8 → 24, 2 → 18, 11 → 19. Under each key move is a diagram showing the pathway of the threads, illustrating how the threads move in a circular movement, one slot at a time. Under the diagram is the full sequence of moves that the threads have to travel to complete the pathway.

The key move appears to the top left of the Maru Dai diagram on each design page.

Key Move

$5 \rightarrow 13$

Pathway

$5 \rightarrow 13$
$4 \rightarrow 5$
$15 \rightarrow 4$
$3 \rightarrow 15$
$2 \rightarrow 3$
$17 \rightarrow 2$
$16 \rightarrow 17$
$15 \rightarrow 16$
$14 \rightarrow 15$
$13 \rightarrow 14$

Key Move

$8 \rightarrow 24$

Pathway

$8 \rightarrow 24$
$9 \rightarrow 8$
$22 \rightarrow 9$
$10 \rightarrow 22$
$11 \rightarrow 10$
$20 \rightarrow 11$
$21 \rightarrow 20$
$22 \rightarrow 21$
$23 \rightarrow 22$
$24 \rightarrow 23$

Key Move

$2 \rightarrow 18$

Pathway

$2 \rightarrow 18$
$3 \rightarrow 2$
$16 \rightarrow 3$
$4 \rightarrow 16$
$5 \rightarrow 4$
$14 \rightarrow 5$
$15 \rightarrow 14$
$16 \rightarrow 15$
$17 \rightarrow 16$
$18 \rightarrow 17$

Key Move

$11 \rightarrow 19$

Pathway

$11 \rightarrow 19$
$10 \rightarrow 11$
$21 \rightarrow 10$
$9 \rightarrow 21$
$8 \rightarrow 9$
$23 \rightarrow 8$
$22 \rightarrow 23$
$21 \rightarrow 22$
$20 \rightarrow 21$
$19 \rightarrow 20$

INVERSION MOVES

The inversion moves shown above the pathway box appear next to the Maru Dai diagrams on each design page. Here, we have pairs of threads that change places with each other. The direction of the arrows indicates which way the threads move – i.e., clockwise or anticlockwise.

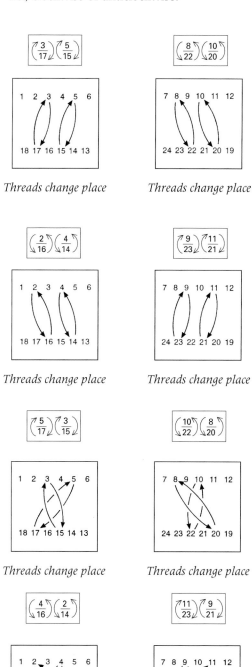

Threads change place

Threads change place

Threads change place

Threads change place

Threads change place

Threads change place

Threads change place

Threads change place

17

PERU

16-strand Braid · *Vertical Stripe with 15 Variations*

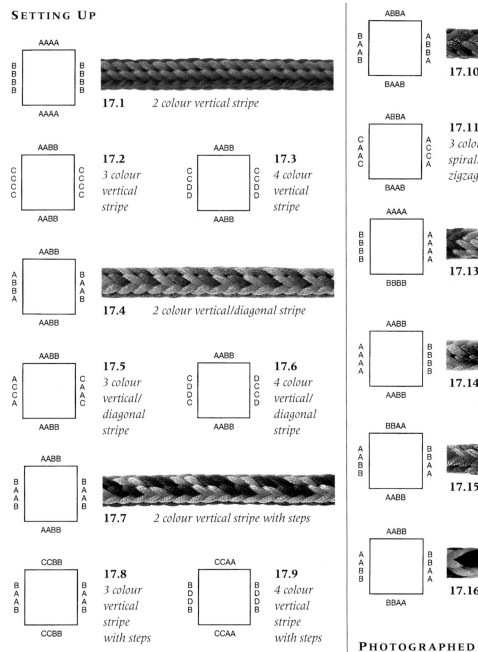

SETTING UP

17.1 *2 colour vertical stripe*

AAAA / BBBB | BBBB / AAAA

17.2 *3 colour vertical stripe*
AABB / CCCC | CCCC / AABB

17.3 *4 colour vertical stripe*
AABB / CCDD | CCDD / AABB

17.4 *2 colour vertical/diagonal stripe*
AABB / ABBA | BAAB / AABB

17.5 *3 colour vertical/diagonal stripe*
AABB / ACCA | CAAC / AABB

17.6 *4 colour vertical/diagonal stripe*
AABB / CDDC | DCCD / AABB

17.7 *2 colour vertical stripe with steps*
AABB / BAAB | BAAB / AABB

17.8 *3 colour vertical stripe with steps*
CCBB / BAAB | BAAB / CCBB

17.9 *4 colour vertical stripe with steps*
CCAA / BDDB | BDDB / CCAA

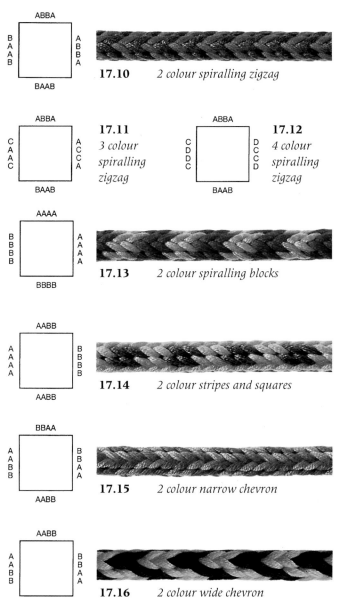

17.10 *2 colour spiralling zigzag*
ABBA / BAAB | ABBA / BAAB

17.11 *3 colour spiralling zigzag*
ABBA / CAAC | ACCA / BAAB

17.12 *4 colour spiralling zigzag*
ABBA / CDDC | DCCD / BAAB

17.13 *2 colour spiralling blocks*
AAAA / BBBB | AAAA / BBBB

17.14 *2 colour stripes and squares*
AABB / AAAA | BBBB / AABB

17.15 *2 colour narrow chevron*
BBAA / AABB | BBAA / AABB

17.16 *2 colour wide chevron*
AABB / AABB | BBAA / BBAA

PHOTOGRAPHED SAMPLES

These were made using: 70gm bobbins / 650gm counter-balance / 15 ends 20/2 cotton.

74

WORKING METHOD

There are two steps to this design. The moves in step 1 are made in a clockwise direction; in step 2 they are anti-clockwise.

To make, continuously repeat steps 1 and 2.

MARU DAI AND CARD

Card method: key move details are shown on page 73.

Home slots   2 3 4 5   8 9 10 11   14 15 16 17   20 21 22 23

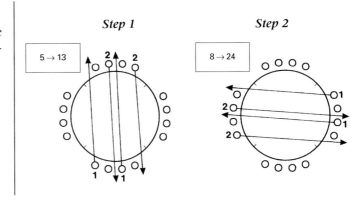

18

PERU

16-strand Braid · *Chevron with 11 Variations*

SETTING UP

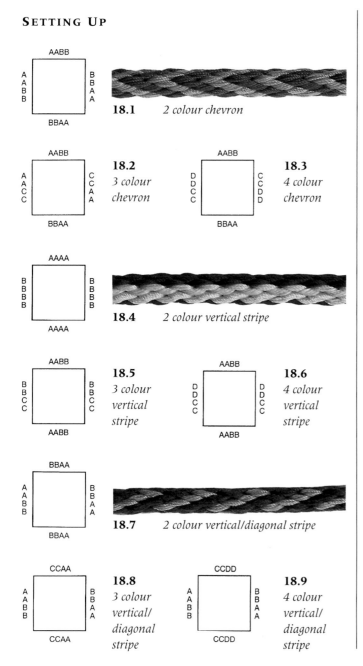

18.1   *2 colour chevron*

18.2   *3 colour chevron*

18.3   *4 colour chevron*

18.4   *2 colour vertical stripe*

18.5   *3 colour vertical stripe*

18.6   *4 colour vertical stripe*

18.7   *2 colour vertical/diagonal stripe*

18.8   *3 colour vertical/diagonal stripe*

18.9   *4 colour vertical/diagonal stripe*

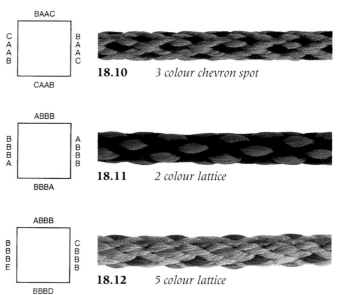

18.10   *3 colour chevron spot*

18.11   *2 colour lattice*

18.12   *5 colour lattice*

PHOTOGRAPHED SAMPLES

These were made using: 70gm bobbins / 650gm counterbalance / 9 ends 35/3 silk.

The two lattice patterns can be enhanced by using thicker threads for the A threads in pattern 18.11 and for the A, C, D and E threads in pattern 18.12.

In Designs 19–26, which follow, the basic steps of Designs 17 and 18 are used in different sequences to create varying diamond and fret designs. The steps in Design 18 reverse the structure, inverting the pattern to give the diamonds and the frets.

WORKING METHOD

Four steps make up the chevron design. With each step, threads change place with each other. Steps 1 and 4 move clockwise; steps 2 and 3 move anticlockwise.

To make, continuously repeat steps 1–4.

76

Maru Dai and Card

Card method: key move details are shown on page 73.

Home slots   2 3 4 5   8 9 10 11   14 15 16 17   20 21 22 23

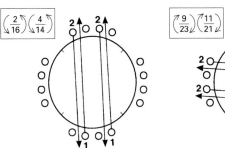
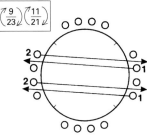

Step 1   ***Step 2***   ***Step 3***   ***Step 4***

16-strand Braid · *Diamond with Four Variations*

SETTING UP

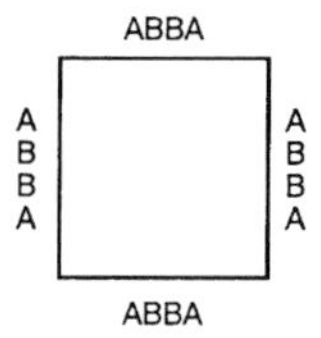

ABBA

A
B
B
A

ABBA

A
B
B
A

19.1   *2 colour diamond*

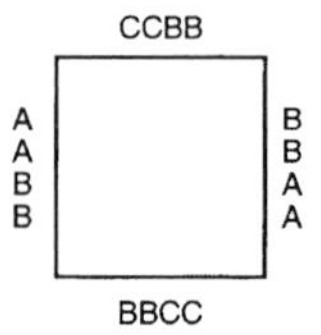

CCBB

A
A
B
B

B
B
A
A

BBCC

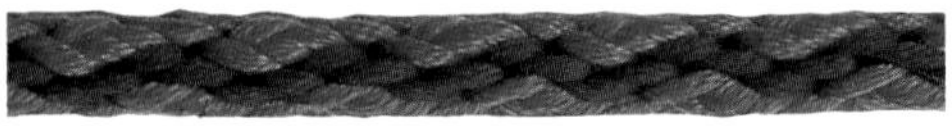

19.2   *3 colour diamond*

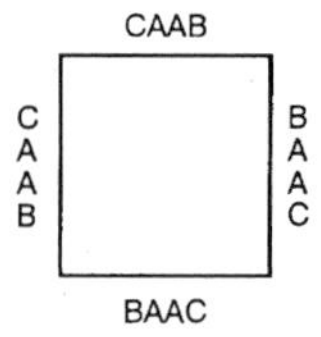

CAAB

C
A
A
B

B
A
A
C

BAAC

19.3   *3 colour rosebud*

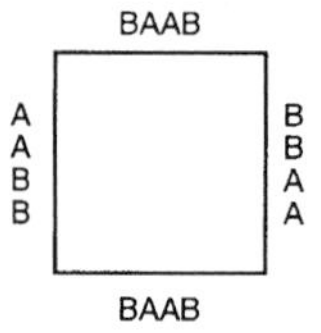

BAAB

A
A
B
B

B
B
A
A

BAAB

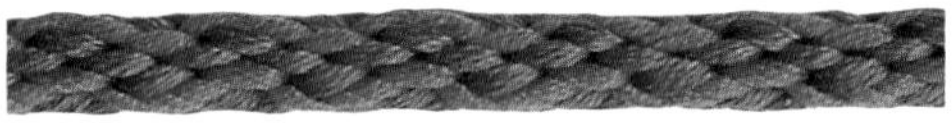

19.4   *2 colour zigzag*

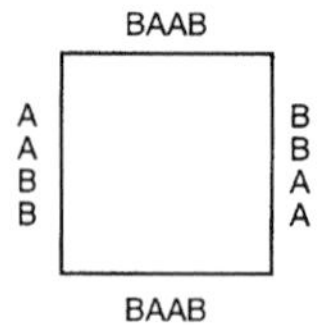

BAAB

A
A
B
B

B
B
A
A

BAAB

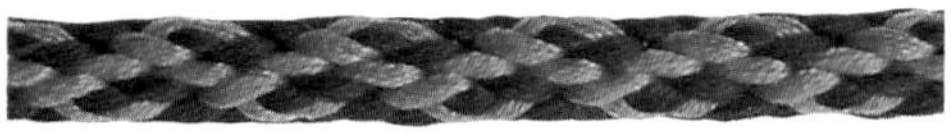

19.5   *2 colour zigzags and hooks*

Suggested colours for the rosebud, pattern 19.3, are A = brown, B = red and C = Green. To give prominence to the rosebud, double the thickness of the red threads.

Patterns 19.4 and 19.5 can both be made with three colours.

PHOTOGRAPHED SAMPLES

These were made using: 70gm bobbins / 540gm counter-balance / 15 ends 20/2 cotton.

WORKING METHOD

Patterns 19.1–19.4 are made in a repeating 8-step sequence shown below.

Pattern 19.5 is made in two stages. Stage 1 consists of 10 steps, the two extra steps in the sequence setting the structure for this pattern. On completion of stage 1 go directly to stage 2.

For stage 2 repeat this sequence of eight steps for the entire length of the braid to maintain the zigzag and hook design.

Pattern	make steps in this sequence
19.1–19.4	1 2 3 4 5 6 7 8 repeat
19.5 stage 1	1 2 3 4 5 6 5 6 7 8 do not repeat, continue with stage 2
stage 2	1 2 3 4 5 6 7 8 repeat

In patterns 19.1 and 19.2 the position of the colour can be reversed. This can be done by following this sequence of steps: 1 2 3 4   5 6 7 8 then 3 4 7 8, then continue with 1 2 3 4   5 6 7 8 for the desired length. To revert to the original colour arrangement, follow this sequence of steps: 1 2 3 4   5 6 7 8   1 2 3 4, then 7 8 3 4   5 6 7 8, then continue with 1 2 3 4   5 6 7 8.

Several changes can be made along the length of the braid.

MARU DAI AND CARD

Make to the sequence of steps shown above in Working Method. Card method: key move details are shown on page 73.

Home slots   2 3 4 5   8 9 10 11   14 15 16 17   20 21 22 23

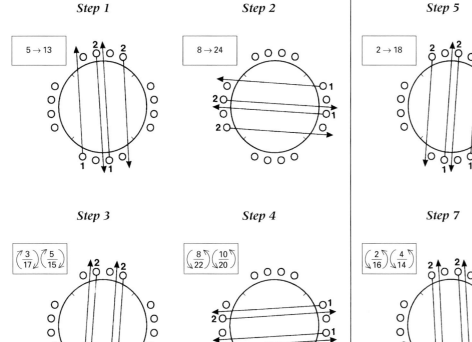

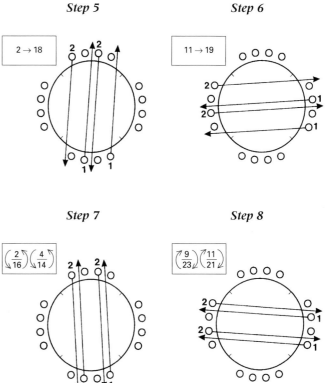

Step 1

5 → 13

Step 2

8 → 24

Step 3

$\left(\dfrac{3}{17}\right)\left(\dfrac{5}{15}\right)$

Step 4

$\left(\dfrac{8}{22}\right)\left(\dfrac{10}{20}\right)$

Step 5

2 → 18

Step 6

11 → 19

Step 7

$\left(\dfrac{2}{16}\right)\left(\dfrac{4}{14}\right)$

Step 8

$\left(\dfrac{9}{23}\right)\left(\dfrac{11}{21}\right)$

20

16-strand Braid · *Fret and Diamond with Three Variations*

SETTING UP

Patterns 20.2, 20.3 and 20.4 use the same setting-up diagram as 20.1.

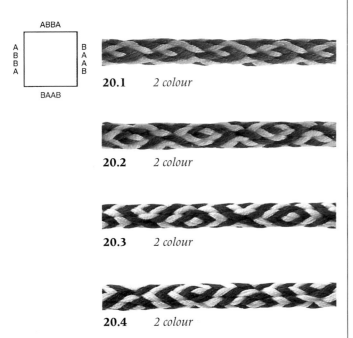

20.1   *2 colour*

20.2   *2 colour*

20.3   *2 colour*

20.4   *2 colour*

Pattern	make steps in this sequence
20.1	1 2 3 4 5 6 7 8 repeat
20.2	1 2 1 2 3 4 5 6 5 6 7 8 repeat
20.3	1 2 1 2 1 2 3 4 5 6 5 6 5 6 7 8 repeat
20.4	1 2 1 2 1 2 1 2 3 4 5 6 5 6 5 6 5 6 7 8 repeat

MARU DAI AND CARD

Make to the sequence of steps shown under Working Method. Card method: key move details are shown on page 73.

Home slots   2 3 4 5   8 9 10 11   14 15 16 17   20 21 22 23

PHOTOGRAPHED SAMPLES

These were made using: 70gm bobbins / 630gm counterbalance / 15 ends 20/2 cotton.

WORKING METHOD

Pattern 20.1 is made by repeating steps 1–8. In patterns 20.2–20.4 the diamond and fret pattern is progressively increased in length by introducing additional steps as follows.

Step 1

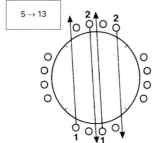

Step 2

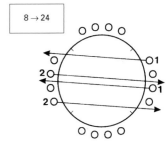

Step 3

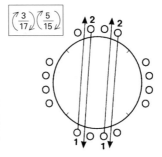

Step 4

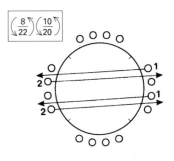

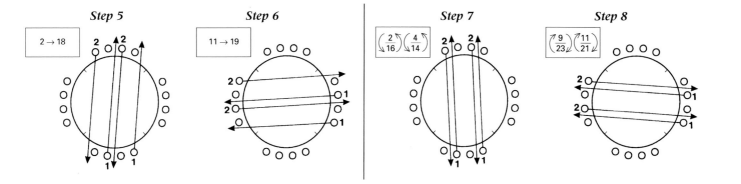

16-strand Braid · *Spiralling Fret with Two Variations*

SETTING UP

Patterns 21.2 and 21.3 use the same setting-up diagram as 21.1.

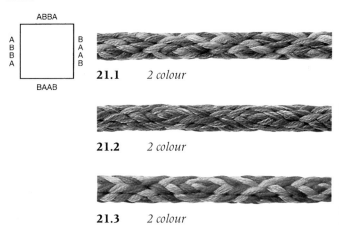

21.1 *2 colour*

21.2 *2 colour*

21.3 *2 colour*

PHOTOGRAPHED SAMPLES

These were made using: 70gm bobbins / 630gm counter-balance / 15 ends 20/2 cotton.

WORKING METHOD

To make the three patterns, complete the steps shown below.

Pattern	*make steps in this sequence*
21.1	12 14 36 5 6 7 8 repeat
21.2	12 1214 36 56 5678 repeat
21.3	1212 1214 36 5656 5678 repeat

MARU DAI AND CARD

Make to the sequence of steps shown under Working Method. Card method: key move details are shown on page 73.

Home slots   2 3 4 5   8 9 10 11   14 15 16 17   20 21 22 23

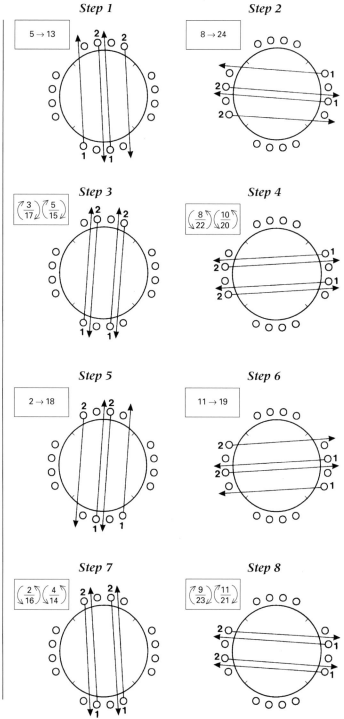

16-strand Braid · *Spiralling Diamond with Two Variations*

SETTING UP

Patterns 22.2 and 22.3 use the same setting-up diagram as 22.1.

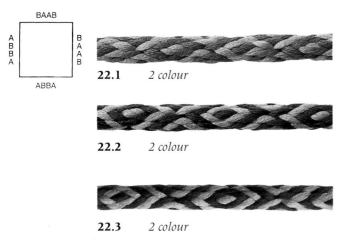

22.1   *2 colour*

22.2   *2 colour*

22.3   *2 colour*

PHOTOGRAPHED SAMPLES

These were made using: 70gm bobbins / 630gm counter-balance / 15 ends 20/2 cotton.

WORKING METHOD

To make the three patterns, complete the steps shown below.

Pattern	make steps in this sequence
22.1	1 2 1 4 3 6 5 6 7 8 repeat
22.2	1 2 1 2 1 4 3 6 5 6 5 6 7 8 repeat
22.3	1 2 1 2 1 2 1 4 3 6 5 6 5 6 5 6 7 8 repeat

MARU DAI AND CARD

Make to the sequence of steps shown under Working Method. Card method: key move details are shown on page 73.

Home slots   2 3 4 5   8 9 10 11   14 15 16 17   20 21 22 23

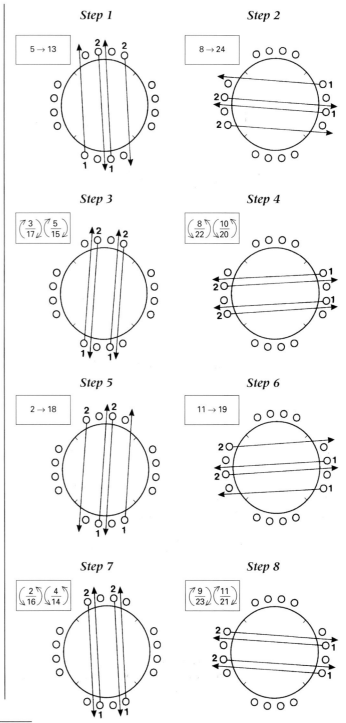

16-strand Braid · *Diamond with Nine Variations*

SETTING UP

Patterns 23.2–23.10 use the same setting-up diagram as 23.1.

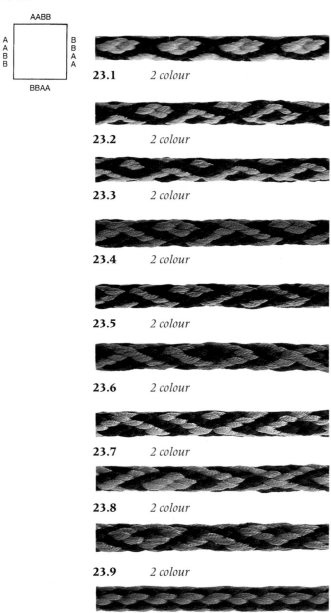

AABB

A A A B B B B A A

BBAA

23.1   *2 colour*

23.2   *2 colour*

23.3   *2 colour*

23.4   *2 colour*

23.5   *2 colour*

23.6   *2 colour*

23.7   *2 colour*

23.8   *2 colour*

23.9   *2 colour*

23.10   *2 colour*

PHOTOGRAPHED SAMPLES

These were made using: 70gm bobbins / 540gm counter-balance / 15 ends 20/2 cotton.

WORKING METHOD

Designs 23, 24 and 25 are all developed from Design 18, the chevron braid. Steps 1–4 are used as the basic moves. To change the chevron pattern into a diamond or fret design, the structure has to be inverted. This is done by introducing new inversion moves, steps 5–8.

There are two Maru Dai diagrams for each inversion step. The key moves for the card method are shown between these diagrams. To make the 10 patterns in Design 23 complete the steps shown below:

Pattern		make steps in this sequence				
23.1		1 2 3 4	5 6 3 4	1 2 7 8	repeat	
23.2		1 2 3 4	1 2 7 8	repeat		
23.3	stage 1	1 2 3 4	1 2 7 8	do not repeat, continue with stage 2		
	stage 2	1 2 3 4	5 6 3 4	1 2 7 8	repeat	
23.4		1 2 3 4	1 2 3 4	5 6 3 4	1 2 3 4	1 2 7 8
		repeat				
23.5		1 2 3 4	1 2 3 4	1 2 7 8	repeat	
23.6		1 2 3 4	1 2 3 4	1 2 3 4	5 6 3 4	1 2 3 4
		1 2 3 4	1 2 7 8		repeat	
23.7		1 2 3 4	1 2 3 4	1 2 3 4	1 2 7 8	repeat
23.8		1 2 3 4	1 2 3 4	1 2 3 4	1 2 3 4	5 6 3 4
		1 2 3 4	1 2 3 4	1 2 3 4	1 2 7 8	repeat
23.9	stage 1	3 4 1 2	3 4 5 6	do not repeat, continue with stage 2		
	stage 2	3 4 1 2	3 4 1 2	7 8 1 2 3 4 1 2 3 4		
		5 6 repeat				
23.10	stage 1	1 2 do not repeat, continue with stage 2				
	stage 2	7 8 5 6	repeat			

84

MARU DAI AND CARD

Make to the sequence of steps shown under Working Method. Card method: key move details are shown on page 73.

Home slots   2 3 4 5   8 9 10 11   14 15 16 17   20 21 22 23

Step 1

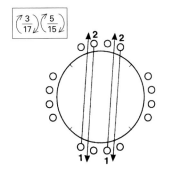

Step 2

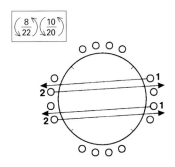

Step 3

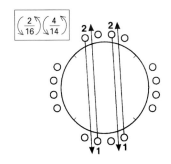

Step 4

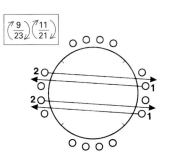

Step 5

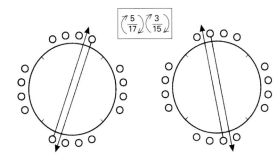

Step 6

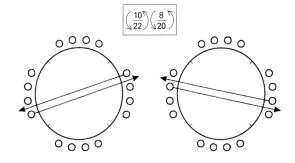

Step 7

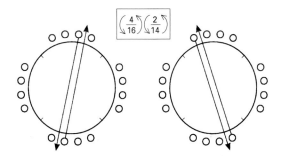

Step 8

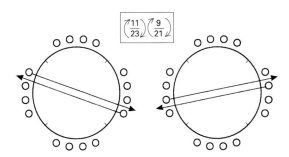

16-strand Braid · *Diamond with Four Variations*

SETTING UP

Patterns 24.2–24.5 use the same setting-up diagram as 24.1.

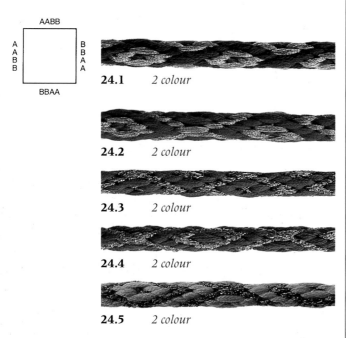

24.1 *2 colour*

24.2 *2 colour*

24.3 *2 colour*

24.4 *2 colour*

24.5 *2 colour*

PHOTOGRAPHED SAMPLES

These were made using: 70gm bobbins / 540gm counter-balance / 15 ends 20/2 cotton.

WORKING METHOD

The diamond patterns in this design are created by moving upper threads (see page 47 for an explanation of lower and upper threads). It is the sequence of steps 1 2 1 2 or 3 4 3 4 that creates the reversal of the structure, and it is in the second pair of steps that upper threads move – i.e., 1 2 lowers move, 1 2 uppers move; 3 4 lowers move; 3 4 uppers move.

Moving the upper threads creates an inversion in the structure, changing the chevron to a diamond. It is not necessary therefore to use the inversion steps 5–8 as in Design 23.

To make the five patterns complete the steps shown below.

Pattern	make steps in this sequence				
24.1	1 2 3 4	1 2 1 2	3 4 1 2	3 4 3 4	repeat
24.2	1 2 3 4	1 2 3 4	1 2 1 2	3 4 1 2	3 4 1 2
	3 4 3 4	repeat			
24.3	1 2 3 4	1 2	3 4 3 4	repeat	
24.4	1 2 3 4	1 2 3 4	1 2	3 4 3 4	repeat
24.5	1 2 3 4	1 2 3 4	1 2 3 4	1 2 1 2	3 4 1 2
	3 4 1 2	3 4 1 2	3 4 3 4	repeat	

MARU DAI AND CARD

Make to the sequence of steps shown under Working Method. Card method: key move details are on page 73.

Home slots   2 3 4 5   8 9 10 11   14 15 16 17   20 21 22 23

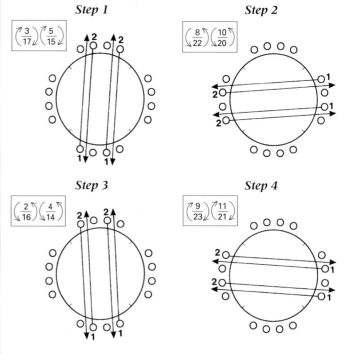

Step 1   *Step 2*

Step 3   *Step 4*

Opposite *This neckpiece, which is made from Design 53, was braided in knitting silks and gold thread. The tassels are threaded with glass beads.*

25

PERU

16-strand Braid · *Fret with Four Variations*

SETTING UP

Patterns 25.2–25.5 use the same setting-up diagram as 25.1.

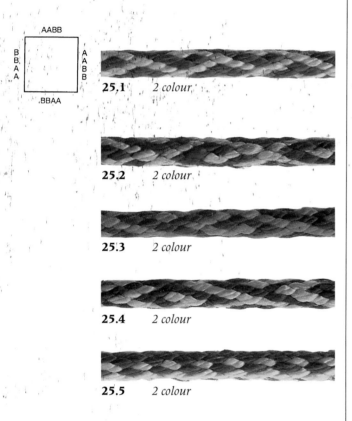

AABB

BBAA

AABB

BBAA

25.1 *2 colour*

25.2 *2 colour*

25.3 *2 colour*

25.4 *2 colour*

25.5 *2 colour*

PHOTOGRAPHED SAMPLES

These were made using: 100gm bobbins / 760gm counter-balance / 1 end 2/2½ silk.

WORKING METHOD

To make the five patterns complete the steps shown below.

Pattern		make steps in this sequence			
25.1		1 2 3 4	5 6 3 4	1 2 7 8	repeat
25.2		1 2 3 4	1 2 7 8	repeat	
25.3		1 2 3 4	1 2 3 4	5 6 3 4	1 2 3 4
		1 2 7 8	repeat		
25.4		1 2 3 4	1 2 3 4	1 2 7 8	repeat
25.5	stage 1	1 2	do not repeat, continue with stage 2		
	stage 2	7 8 5 6	repeat		

MARU DAI AND CARD

Make to the sequence of steps shown under Working Method. Card method: key move details are shown on page 73.

Home slots   2 3 4 5   8 9 10 11   14 15 16 17   20 21 22 23

Step 1   *Step 2*

Step 3

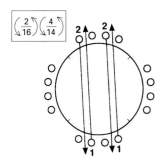

Step 4

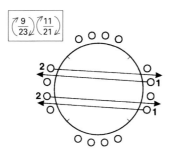

Step 7

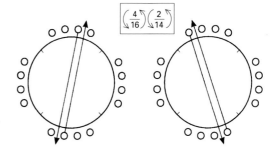

Step 5

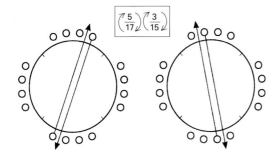

Step 8

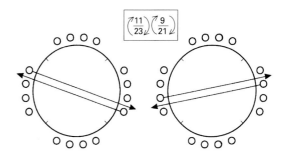

Step 6

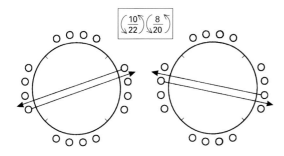

16-strand Braid · *Spiral with Three Variations*

SETTING UP

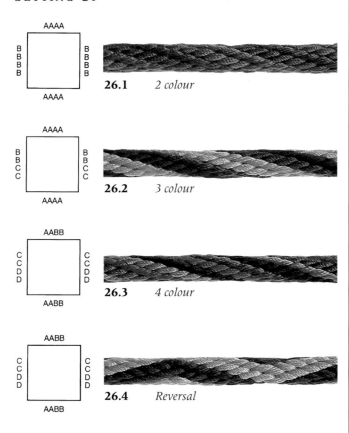

26.1   *2 colour*

26.2   *3 colour*

26.3   *4 colour*

26.4   *Reversal*

PHOTOGRAPHED SAMPLES

These were made using: 70gm bobbins / 540gm counter-balance / 8 ends 30/3 silk.

WORKING METHOD

This method of making the spiral braid is known in Peru and Tibet. It is a different structure from the Japanese spiral shown in Design 45. To make the patterns spiral in one direction only, continuously repeat steps 1 and 2.

Before you can make a pattern in which the direction of the spiral alternates in a clockwise and anticlockwise direction, the structure of the braid has to be changed. This is described below.

REVERSING THE SPIRAL

The following instructions apply to both the Maru Dai and the card methods. Before reversing, the braid moves from steps 1 and 2, which turn clockwise, to steps 3 and 4, which turn anticlockwise. Change each pair of threads (as shown in Fig. 40) and lift the right-hand upper threads over the lower threads to reverse their position.

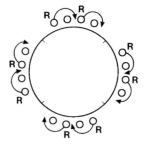

Fig. 40

When the pairs of threads have been changed, continue braiding, repeating steps 3 and 4.

To change back to steps 1 and 2, change each pair of threads (as shown in Fig. 41), lifting the left-hand upper threads over the lower threads.

Fig. 41

MARU DAI AND CARD

To make, continuously repeat steps 1 and 2 for a clockwise spiral, or repeat steps 3 and 4 for an anticlockwise spiral. Card method: key moves are shown on page 73.

Home slots   2 3 4 5   8 9 10 11   14 15 16 17   20 21 22 23

Step 1	*Step 2*	*Step 3*	*Step 4*

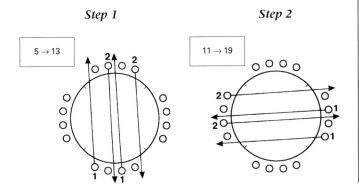

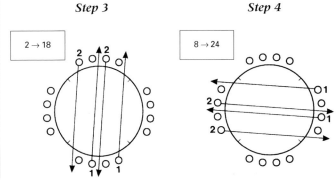

16-strand Braid · *Vertical Stripe with Three Variations*

SETTING UP

This design produces a square-sectioned braid with distinct ridges at each corner. Many more colour combinations can be created, and the texture can be varied by using thicker threads for the corner ridges.

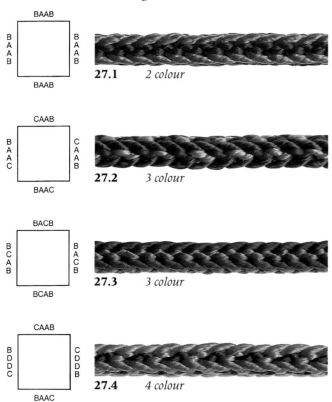

27.1   *2 colour*

27.2   *3 colour*

27.3   *3 colour*

27.4   *4 colour*

PHOTOGRAPHED SAMPLES

These were made using: 70gm bobbins / 450gm counter-balance / 3 ends lyra silk.

WORKING METHOD

PREPARE THE MARU DAI

Wrap towelling around the legs of the Maru Dai as shown in Design 10. Spin the two centre bobbins on all four

sides, as shown in Fig. 42. The north-south bobbins have a Z twist; east-west bobbins are spun with an S twist.

To make, continuously repeat steps 1–4.

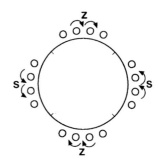

Fig. 42

MARU DAI

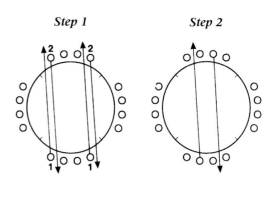

Step 1   *Step 2*

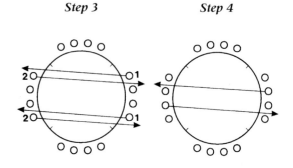

Step 3   *Step 4*

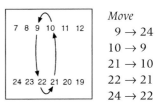

CARD

Home slots   2 3 4 5   8 9 10 11   14 15 16 17   20 21 22 23

Step 1	**Step 2**
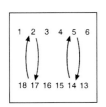	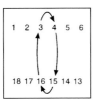
Threads change place	*Pathway*

Move

4 → 13
3 → 4
16 → 3
15 → 16
13 → 15

Step 3	**Step 4**
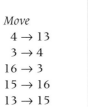	
Threads change place	*Pathway*

Move

9 → 24
10 → 9
21 → 10
22 → 21
24 → 22

28

UK

16-strand Braid · *Spiralling Stripes with Three Variations*

SETTING UP

BAAB
BAAB | | BAAB
BAAB

28.1 *2 colour*

CAAB
BAAC | | CAAB
BAAC

28.2 *3 colour*

BACB
BCAB | | BACB
BCAB

28.3 *3 colour*

CAAB
BDDC | | CDDB
BAAC

28.4 *4 colour*

PHOTOGRAPHED SAMPLES

These were made using: 70gm bobbins / 450gm counterbalance / 20 ends 2/60 cotton.

The setting-up patterns for this design are exactly the same as for Design 27. This spiral design is unusual and attractive and, as with Design 27, thick and thin threads can be used.

WORKING METHOD

It is not necessary to put a twist in the centre bobbins as it was with Design 27.

To make, continuously repeat steps 1–4.

MARU DAI

Step 1
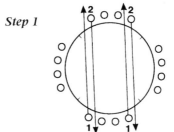

Step 2
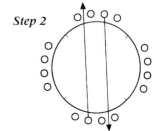

Step 3
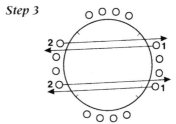

Step 4
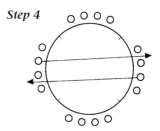

CARD

Home slots   2 3 4 5   8 9 10 11   14 15 16 17   20 21 22 23

Step 1
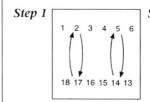

Threads change place

Step 2
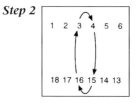

Pathway

Move
4 → 13
3 → 4
16 → 3
15 → 16
13 → 15

Step 3
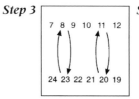

Threads change place

Step 4
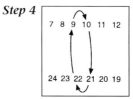

Pathway

Move
10 → 19
9 → 10
22 → 9
21 → 22
19 → 21

16-strand Braid · *Crimped Stripe with Three Variations*

SETTING UP

AAAA
B   B
B   B
B   B
AAAA

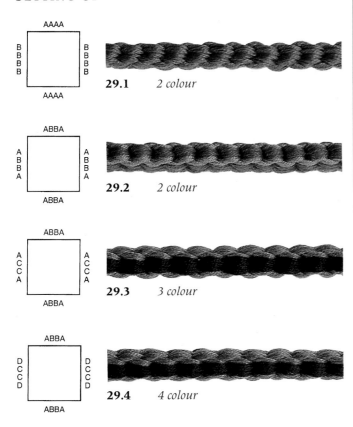

29.1   *2 colour*

ABBA
A   A
B   B
B   B
A   A
ABBA

29.2   *2 colour*

ABBA
A   A
C   C
C   C
A   A
ABBA

29.3   *3 colour*

ABBA
D   D
C   C
C   C
D   D
ABBA

29.4   *4 colour*

PHOTOGRAPHED SAMPLES

These were made using: 70gm bobbins / 450gm counter-balance / 15 ends 20/2 cotton.

WORKING METHOD

The structure of this braid was developed from Design 18. It produces an attractive sectioned braid with a surface texture. As with Designs 27 and 28, not all possible colour variations have been shown.

To make, continuously repeat steps 1–4.

MARU DAI

Step 1

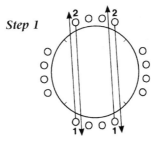

Step 2

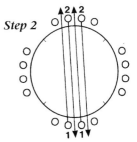

Step 3

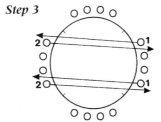

Step 4

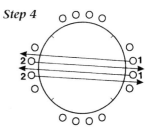

CARD

Home slots   2 3 4 5   8 9 10 11   14 15 16 17   20 21 22 23

Step 1

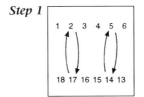

Threads change place

Step 2

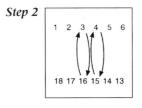

Threads change place

Step 3

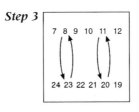

Threads change place

Step 4

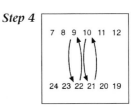

Threads change place

16-strand Braid · *Zigzag with 11 Variations*

SETTING UP

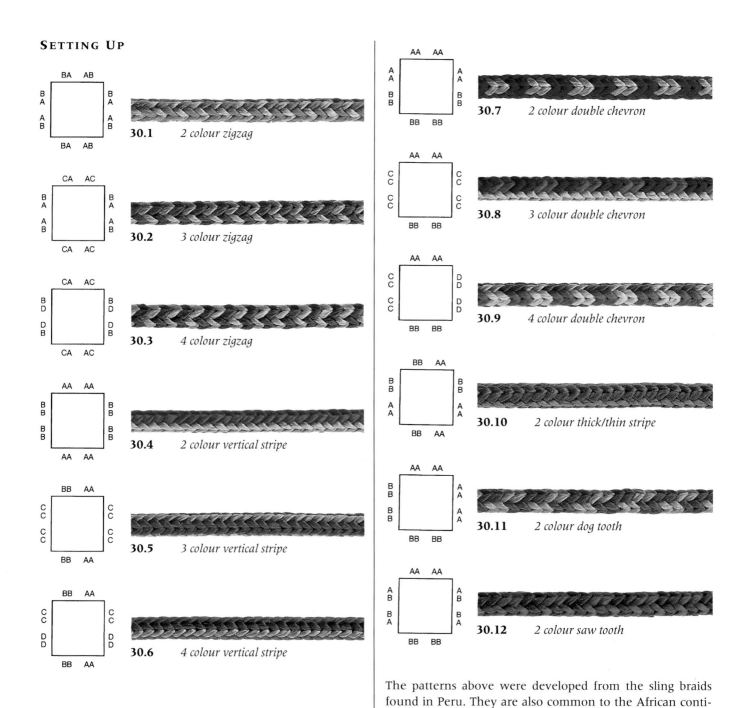

30.1   *2 colour zigzag*

30.2   *3 colour zigzag*

30.3   *4 colour zigzag*

30.4   *2 colour vertical stripe*

30.5   *3 colour vertical stripe*

30.6   *4 colour vertical stripe*

30.7   *2 colour double chevron*

30.8   *3 colour double chevron*

30.9   *4 colour double chevron*

30.10   *2 colour thick/thin stripe*

30.11   *2 colour dog tooth*

30.12   *2 colour saw tooth*

The patterns above were developed from the sling braids found in Peru. They are also common to the African continent and are known in Japan as Maru Genji.

PHOTOGRAPHED SAMPLES

These were made using: 70gm bobbins / 540gm counter-balance / 2 ends lyra silk.

WORKING METHOD

The following making instructions apply to all 12 patterns.

MARU DAI

To make by Maru Dai, continuously repeat steps 1–4.

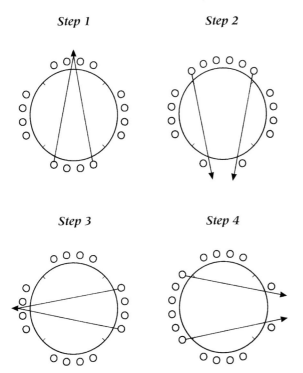

Step 1   *Step 2*

Step 3   *Step 4*

CARD

To make by card, continuously repeat steps 1 and 2.

Home slots   1 2 5 6   7 8 11 12   13 14 17 18   19 20 23 24

Thread the card, leaving slots empty at 3, 4, 9, 10, 15, 16, 21 and 22.

Step 1

```
 1  2  3  4  5  6



18 17 16 15 14 13
```

Pathway

Move
13 → 4
18 → 3
1 → 16
6 → 15

Reposition
2 → 1
3 → 2
5 → 6
4 → 5
14 → 13
15 → 14
17 → 18
16 → 17

Step 2

```
 7  8  9 10 11 12



24 23 22 21 20 19
```

Pathway

Move
19 → 10
24 → 9
7 → 22
12 → 21

Reposition
8 → 7
9 → 8
11 → 12
10 → 11
20 → 19
21 → 20
23 → 24
22 → 23

Flat Braids

This section contains two types of flat braids. The first gives Designs 31–38, and the second gives Designs 39–43.

DESIGNS 31–38

These are made by working two 16-strand braids together to give a 24-strand braid. These designs are extensions of Designs 17–23 and Design 30. This type of flat braid can be made wider still by adding further sets of eight strands to the north-south side of the the setting-up arrangements – see the example below, which shows how the threads for a 24-strand and 32-strand braid are arranged.

24 strand

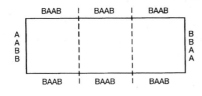

32 strand

MARU DAI

Maru Dai diagrams for Designs 31–38 will be familiar. They are the same moves as were used for the 16-strand braids. The north/south moves are repeated first on the left group and then on the right group. The east/west moves are the same as for the 16-strand counterpart.

CARD

Key move boxes for the card are shown next to the Maru Dai diagrams, in the same way as for the 16-strand braids.

Designs 31–38 use a rectangular card (see Fig. 17a, page 35, for details). The numbered slots are arranged to represent two 16-strand braids side-by-side. The key move for these flat braids corresponds to the 16-strand braid from which they are developed. See key move details on page 73. The north/south moves are repeated twice before working the east/west moves.

DESIGNS 39–43

These represent a completely new group of designs, and they use a square card (see Fig. 17b, page 35, for details). The braids made on this card have different structures from those of Designs 31–38, and they have their own unique sequence of moves. The Maru Dai and card moves are shown in detail for each design.

Remember to work the north/south moves with the south side held to the body, and to work east/west moves with the west side of the body.

TENSION ADJUSTMENT FOR THE MARU DAI AND CARD

To give flat braids a firm finish with an even pattern, it is necessary to control the tension. This is done by adjusting and tightening the east/west threads as they are moved. On the Maru Dai tensioning can be helped by using heavier bobbins for the east/west threads. Guidance on weights is given for each design.

Opposite   Designs 18 and 32 were worked in knitting silks to make this necklace, which is secured with a silver finding and decorated with water pearls, which were stitched onto the finished braid.

24-strand Spiral Braid · *Vertical Stripe with 11 Variations*

SETTING UP

Other patterns can be made by altering the layout of the north/south strands – for example, pattern 31.2 could be changed to A A B B B B A A or to A B B A A B B A, giving two new patterns.

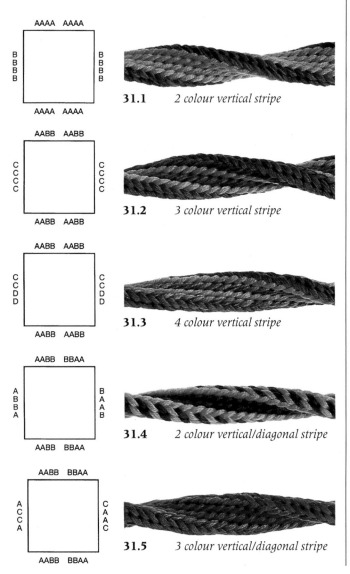

31.1 *2 colour vertical stripe*

31.2 *3 colour vertical stripe*

31.3 *4 colour vertical stripe*

31.4 *2 colour vertical/diagonal stripe*

31.5 *3 colour vertical/diagonal stripe*

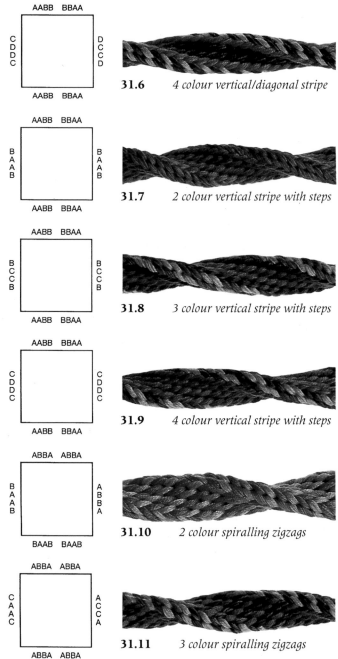

31.6 *4 colour vertical/diagonal stripe*

31.7 *2 colour vertical stripe with steps*

31.8 *3 colour vertical stripe with steps*

31.9 *4 colour vertical stripe with steps*

31.10 *2 colour spiralling zigzags*

31.11 *3 colour spiralling zigzags*

31.12 *4 colour spiralling zigzags*

PHOTOGRAPHED SAMPLES

These were made using: 70gm bobbins / 620gm counterbalance / 15 ends cotton.

WORKING METHOD

To make, continuously repeat steps 1 and 2.

Maru Dai tension can be controlled either by using bobbins of one weight, reducing the counterbalance weight and taking extra care in tightening the east/west threads as they are worked; or by using bobbins of two weights: 100gm on the east/west side and 70gm on the north/south side.

Card method tension relies on tightening the lower east/west threads before they are moved to their new position.

Note: When cutting the threads, allow up to 30 per cent extra in length for the east/west threads.

MARU DAI AND CARD

Card method: key move details are shown on page 73.

Home slots   2 3 4 5   8 9 10 11   14 15 16 17   20 21 22 23

Step 1

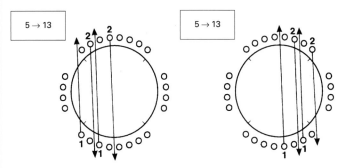

Step 2

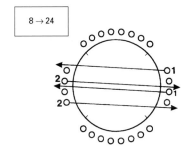

24-strand Flat Braid · *Chevron with 11 Variations*

SETTING UP

Use the 12 setting-up patterns in Design 18 and add eight extra strands. Arrange them in a repeat pattern, four to the north and four to the south, as in the example below.

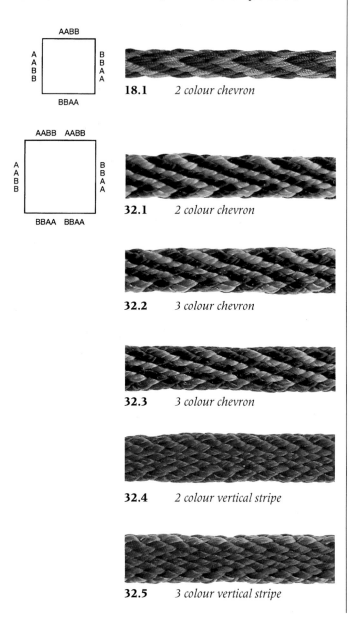

18.1 *2 colour chevron*

32.1 *2 colour chevron*

32.2 *3 colour chevron*

32.3 *3 colour chevron*

32.4 *2 colour vertical stripe*

32.5 *3 colour vertical stripe*

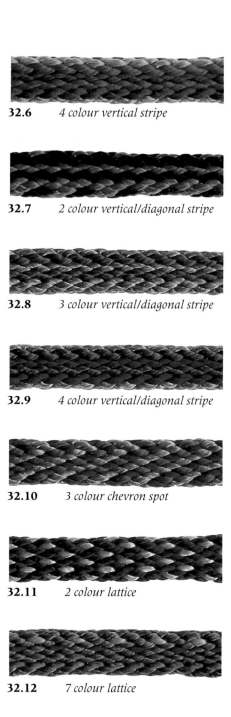

32.6 *4 colour vertical stripe*

32.7 *2 colour vertical/diagonal stripe*

32.8 *3 colour vertical/diagonal stripe*

32.9 *4 colour vertical/diagonal stripe*

32.10 *3 colour chevron spot*

32.11 *2 colour lattice*

32.12 *7 colour lattice*

PHOTOGRAPHED SAMPLES

These were made using: 70gm bobbins / 760gm counter-balance / 2 ends lyra silk.

WORKING METHOD

To make, continuously repeat steps 1–4.

Maru Dai tension can be controlled either by using 24 bobbins all the same weight with a counterbalance of about 45 per cent of the total bobbin weight; or by using 100gm bobbins on the east/west side and 70gm on the north/south side.

Card method tensioning relies on tightening the lower east/west threads before they are moved to their new position.

Note: When cutting the threads, allow up to 50 per cent extra in length for the east/west threads.

MARU DAI AND CARD

Card method: key move details are shown on page 73.

Home slots   2 3 4 5   8 9 10 11   14 15 16 17   20 21 22 23

Step 1

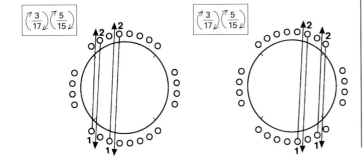

Step 2

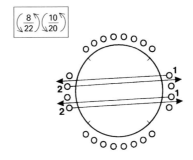

Step 3

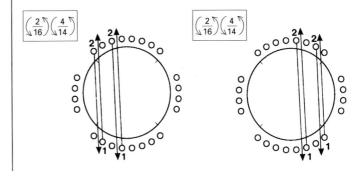

Step 4

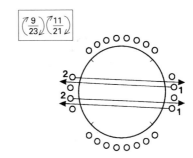

24-strand Flat Braid · *Diamond with Four Variations*

SETTING UP

Use the five setting-up patterns in Design 19, and add extra strands. Arrange them in a repeat pattern, four to the north and four to the south, as in the example below.

19.4   *2 colour zigzag*

33.1   *2 colour diamond*

33.2   *3 colour diamond*

33.3   *3 colour rosebud*

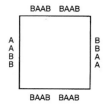

33.4   *2 colour zigzag*

33.5   *2 colour zigzag and hooks*

Pattern 33.2 can also be arranged in a sequence A B B C C B B A, giving a pattern with a central wavy line with diamonds on the edge. In pattern 33.3 make a design with rosebuds on both edges of the braid by arranging the threads to look like this:

North   C B B A A B B A
South   A B B A A B B C

Suggested colours for the rosebud are A = Red, B = Brown and C = Green.

PHOTOGRAPHED SAMPLES

These were made using: 70gm bobbins / 620gm counter-balance / 9 ends 30/3 silk.

WORKING METHOD

Patterns 33.1–33.4 are made in a repeating 8 step sequence. Pattern 33.5 is made in two stages, and there are two extra steps in the stage 1 sequence, which is made only once at the beginning of the braid. Stage 2 is then repeated for the length of the braid.

Pattern		make steps in this sequence
33.1–33.4		1 2 3 4 5 6 7 8 repeat
33.5	stage 1	1 2 3 4 5 6 5 6 7 8 do not repeat, continue with stage 2
	stage 2	1 2 3 4 5 6 7 8 repeat

Maru Dai tension can be controlled either by using 24 bobbins all the same weight with a counterbalance of about 37 per cent of total bobbin weight; or by using 100gm bobbins on the east/west side and 70gm on the north/south side.

Card method tensioning relies on tightening the lower east/west threads before they are moved to their new positions.

Note: When cutting the threads allow up to 30 per cent extra in length for the east/west threads.

MARU DAI AND CARD

Make to the sequence of steps shown under Working Method. Card method: key move details are shown on page 73.

Home slots   2 3 4 5   8 9 10 11   14 15 16 17   20 21 22 23

Step 1

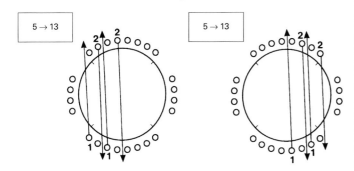

Step 2

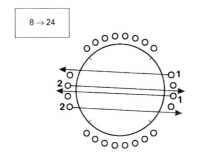

Step 3

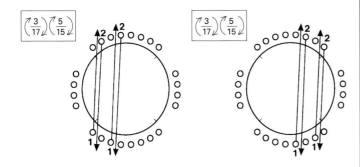

Step 4

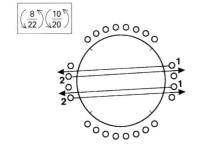

Step 5

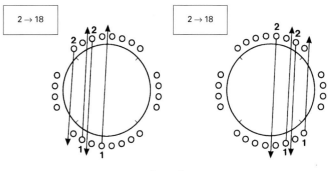

Step 6

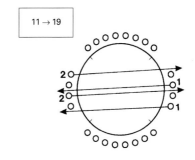

Step 7

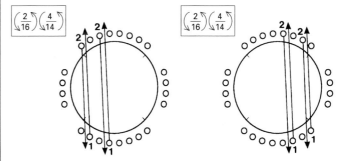

Step 8

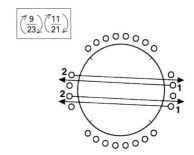

24-strand Flat Braid · *Fret and Diamond with Three Variations*

SETTING UP

This design is a development of Design 20. Patterns 34.2–34.4 use the same setting-up diagram as 34.1.

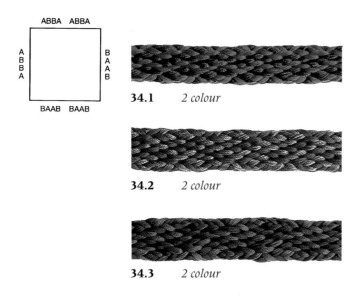

34.1   *2 colour*

34.2   *2 colour*

34.3   *2 colour*

34.4   *2 colour*

PHOTOGRAPHED SAMPLES

These were made using: 70gm bobbins / 710gm counterbalance / 8 ends 40/3 silk.

WORKING METHOD

Pattern 34.1 is made by repeating steps 1–8. In patterns 34.2–34.4 the diamond and fret pattern is progressively increased in length by introducing additional steps as follows.

Pattern	make steps in this sequence
34.1	1 2 3 4 5 6 7 8 repeat
34.2	1 2 1 2 3 4 5 6 5 6 7 8 repeat
34.3	1 2 1 2 1 2 3 4 5 6 5 6 5 6 7 8 repeat
34.4	1 2 1 2 1 2 1 2 3 4 5 6 5 6 5 6 5 6 7 8 repeat

Maru Dai tension can be controlled either by using 24 bobbins all the same weight with a counterbalance of about 42 per cent of total bobbin weight; or by using 100gm bobbins on the east/west side and 70gm on the north/south side.

Card method tensioning relies on tightening the lower east/west threads before they are moved to their new position.

Note: When cutting the threads allow up to 50 per cent extra in length for the east/west threads.

MARU DAI AND CARD

Make to the sequence of steps shown under Working Method. Card method: key move details are shown on page 73.

Home slots   2 3 4 5   8 9 10 11   14 15 16 17   20 21 22 23

Step 1

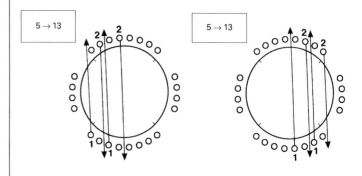

Step 2

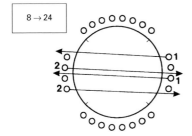

Step 5

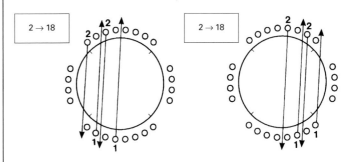

Step 3

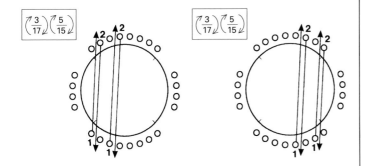

Step 6

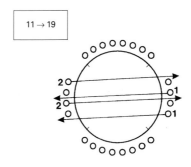

Step 4

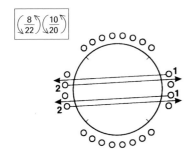

Step 7

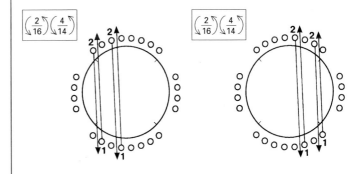

Step 8

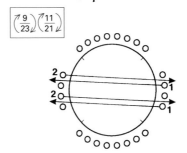

24-strand Flat Braid · *Spiralling Diamond with Two Variations*

SETTING UP

This design is a development of Design 21. Patterns 35.2 and 35.3 use the same setting-up diagram as 35.1.

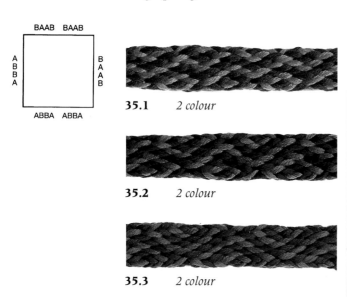

35.1   *2 colour*

35.2   *2 colour*

35.3   *2 colour*

PHOTOGRAPHED SAMPLES

These were made using: 70gm bobbins / 710gm counter-balance / 3 ends Madeira sixtwist.

WORKING METHOD

To make the three patterns, complete the steps shown below.

Pattern	make steps in this sequence
35.1	1 2 1 4 3 6 5 6 7 8 repeat
35.2	1 2 1 2 1 4 3 6 5 6 5 6 7 8 repeat
35.3	1 2 1 2 1 2 1 4 3 6 5 6 5 6 5 6 7 8 repeat

Maru Dai tension can be controlled either by using 24 bobbins all the same weight with a counterbalance of about 42 per cent of total bobbin weight; or by using 100gm bobbins on the east/west side and 70gm on the north/south side.

Card method tensioning relies on tightening the lower east/west threads before they are moved to their new position.

Note: When cutting the threads allow up to 30 per cent extra in length for the east/west threads.

MARU DAI AND CARD

Make to the sequence of steps shown under Working Method. Card method: key move details are shown on page 73.

Home slots   2 3 4 5   8 9 10 11   14 15 16 17   20 21 22 23

Step 1

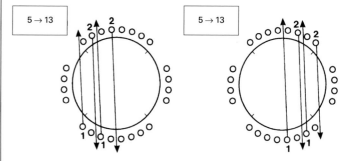

Step 2

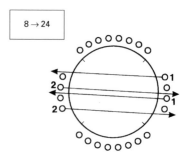

Step 3

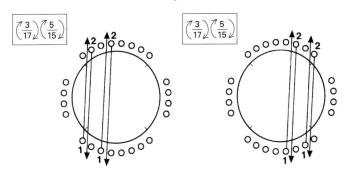

Step 4

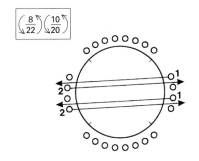

Step 5

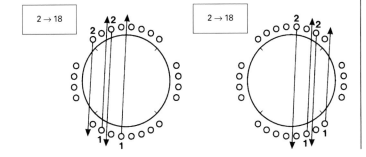

Step 6

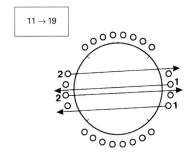

Step 7

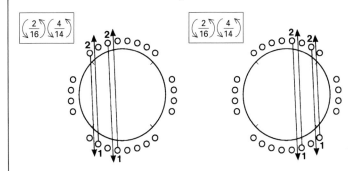

Step 8

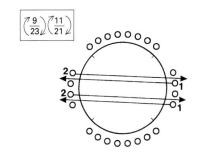

36

PERU

24-strand Flat Braid · *Spiralling Fret with Two Variations*

SETTING UP

This design is a development of Design 22. Patterns 36.2 and 36.3 use the same setting-up diagram as 36.1.

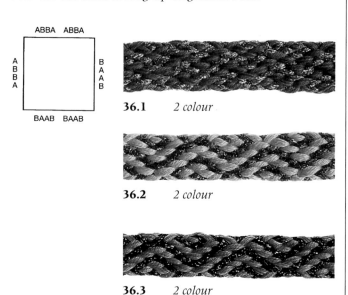

36.1   *2 colour*

36.2   *2 colour*

36.3   *2 colour*

PHOTOGRAPHED SAMPLES

These were made using: 70gm bobbins / 620gm counter-balance / 12 ends 20/2 cotton.

WORKING METHOD

To make the three patterns, complete the steps shown below.

Pattern	*make steps in this sequence*
36.1	1 2 1 4 3 6 5 6 7 8 repeat
36.2	1 2 1 2 1 4 3 6 5 6 5 6 7 8 repeat
36.3	1 2 1 2 1 2 1 4 3 6 5 6 5 6 5 6 7 8 repeat

Maru Dai tension can be controlled either by using 24 bobbins all the same weight with a counterbalance of about 37 per cent of total bobbin weight; or by using 100gm bobbins on the east/west side and 70gm on the north/south side.

Card method tensioning relies on tightening the lower east/west threads before they are moved to their new position.

Note: When cutting the threads allow up to 30 per cent extra in length for the east/west threads.

MARU DAI AND CARD

Make to the sequence of steps shown under Working Method. Card method: key move details are shown on page 73.

Home slots   2 3 4 5   8 9 10 11   14 15 16 17   20 21 22 23

Step 1

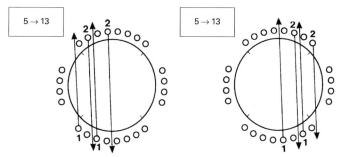

Step 2

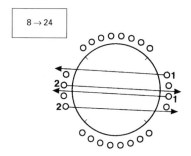

110

Step 3

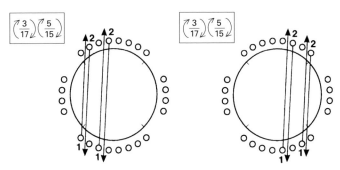

Step 4

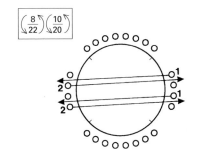

Step 5

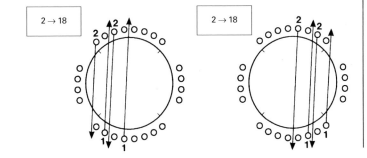

Step 6

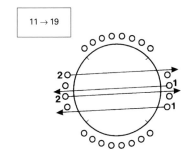

Step 7

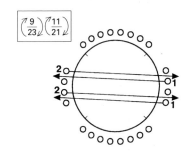

Step 8

37

24-strand Flat Braid · *Diamond with Nine Variations*

SETTING UP

This design is a development of Design 23. Patterns 37.2–37.10 use the same setting-up diagram as 37.1

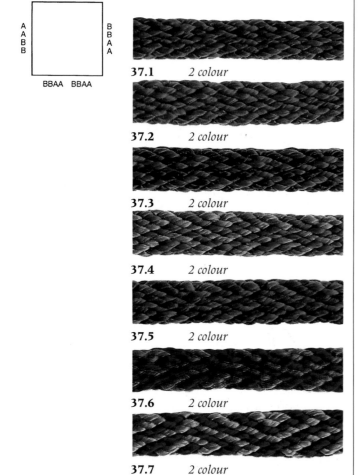

37.1   *2 colour*

37.2   *2 colour*

37.3   *2 colour*

37.4   *2 colour*

37.5   *2 colour*

37.6   *2 colour*

37.7   *2 colour*

37.8   *2 colour*

37.9   *2 colour*

37.10   *2 colour*

PHOTOGRAPHED SAMPLES

These were made using: 70gm bobbins / 620gm counter-balance / 2 ends lyra silk.

WORKING METHOD

Design 37 is a progression from Design 23, Design 18 and Design 5, the 8-strand chevron braid. To change the chevron pattern into a diamond design the structure has to be inverted. For this design it is changed by introducing new inversion moves (see steps 5–8 in this design in the Maru Dai and card moves). To make the 10 patterns in Design 37, complete the steps shown below:

Pattern		make steps in this sequence				
37.1		1 2 3 4	5 6 3 4	1 2 7 8	repeat	
37.2		1 2 3 4	1 2 7 8	repeat		
37.3	stage 1	1 2 3 4	1 2 7 8	do not repeat, continue with stage 2		
	stage 2	1 2 3 4	5 6 3 4	1 2 7 8	repeat	
37.4		1 2 3 4	1 2 3 4	5 6 3 4	1 2 3 4	
		1 2 7 8	repeat			
37.5		1 2 3 4	1 2 3 4	1 2 7 8	repeat	
37.6		1 2 3 4	1 2 3 4	1 2 3 4	5 6 3 4	1 2 3 4
		1 2 3 4	1 2 7 8	repeat		
37.7		1 2 3 4	1 2 3 4	1 2 3 4	1 2 7 8	repeat
37.8		1 2 3 4	1 2 3 4	1 2 3 4	1 2 3 4	5 6 3 4
		1 2 3 4	1 2 3 4	1 2 3 4	1 2 7 8	repeat
37.9	stage 1	3 4 1 2	3 4 5 6	do not repeat, continue with stage 2		
	stage 2	3 4 1 2	3 4 1 2	7 8	1 2 3 4	1 2 3 4
		5 6	repeat			

112

37.10 stage 1   1 2   do not repeat, continue with stage 2

stage 2   7 8 5 6   repeat

Maru Dai tension can be controlled either by using 24 bob-bins all the same weight with a counterbalance of about 37 per cent of total bobbin weight; or by using 100gm bobbins on the east/west side and 70gm on the north/south side.

Card method tensioning relies on tightening the lower east/west threads before they are moved.

Note: When cutting the threads allow up to 50 per cent extra in length for the east/west threads.

MARU DAI AND CARD

Make to the sequence of steps shown under Working Method. Card method: key move details are shown on page 73.

Home slots   2 3 4 5   8 9 10 11   14 15 16 17   20 21 22 23

Step 1

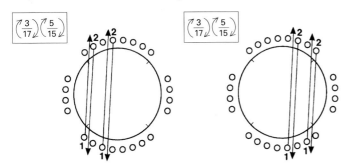

Step 2

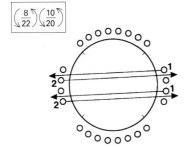

Step 3

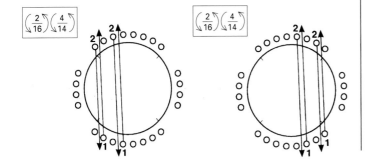

Step 4

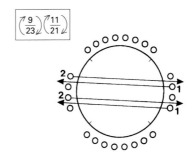

Step 5

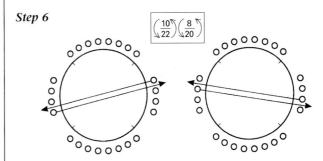

Step 6

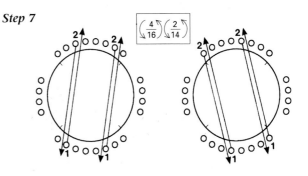

Step 7

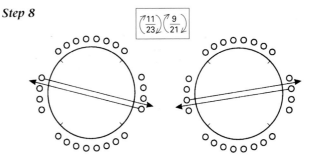

Step 8

24-strand Flat Braid · *Zigzag Design with 10 Variations*

SETTING UP

This design is a development of Design 30.

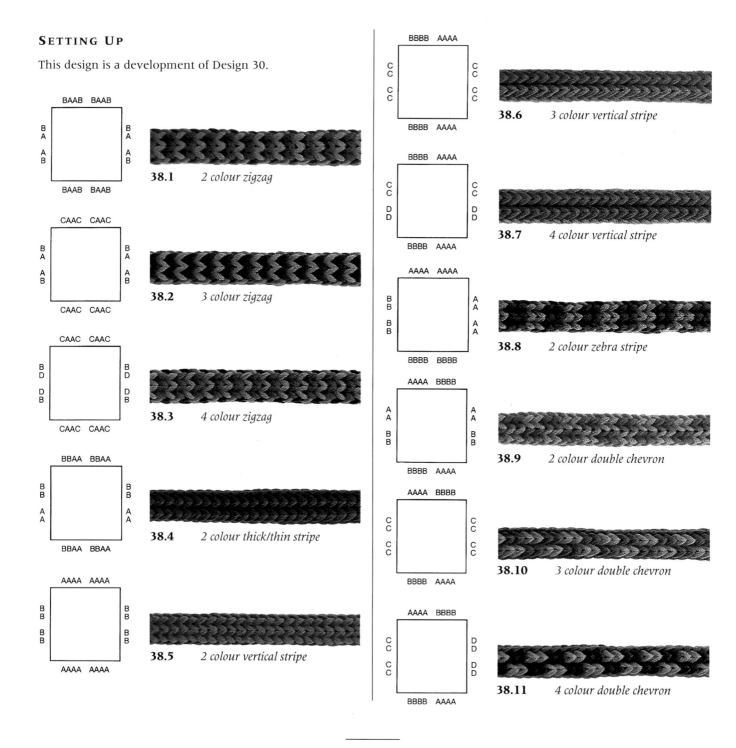

BAAB BAAB

B   B
A   A
A   A
B   B

BAAB BAAB

38.1   *2 colour zigzag*

38.2   *3 colour zigzag*

38.3   *4 colour zigzag*

38.4   *2 colour thick/thin stripe*

38.5   *2 colour vertical stripe*

38.6   *3 colour vertical stripe*

38.7   *4 colour vertical stripe*

38.8   *2 colour zebra stripe*

38.9   *2 colour double chevron*

38.10   *3 colour double chevron*

38.11   *4 colour double chevron*

PHOTOGRAPHED SAMPLES

These were made using: 70gm bobbins / 620gm counterbalance / 6 ends 30/3 silk.

WORKING METHOD

The following making instructions apply to all 11 patterns.

Maru Dai tension can be controlled either by using 24 bobbins all the same weight with a counterbalance of about 37 per cent of total bobbin weight; or by using 100gm bobbins on the east/west side and 70gm on the north/south side.

Card method tensioning relies on tightening the lower east/west threads before they are moved to their new position.

Note: When cutting the threads allow up to 50 per cent extra in length for the east/west threads.

MARU DAI

To make by Maru Dai, continuously repeat steps 1–6.

After finishing step 6, tighten the lower east/west threads before proceeding to step 1. This closes up the north/south threads so that the east/west threads do not show.

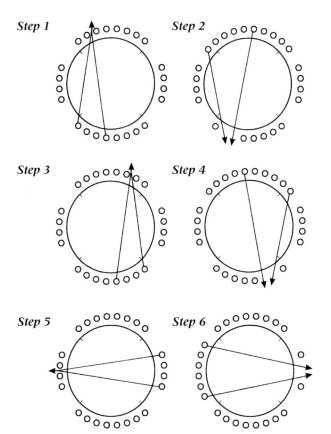

CARD

To make by card, continuously repeat steps 1 and 2.

Home slots   1 2   5 6   7 8   11 12   13 14   17 18   19 20 23 24

Thread the card, leaving slots empty at 3, 4, 9, 10, 15, 16, 21 and 22.

Step 1

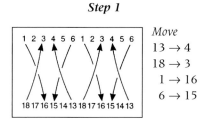

Move
13 → 4
18 → 3
1 → 16
6 → 15

Pathway

Step 2

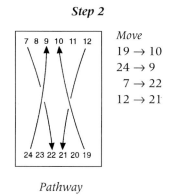

Move
19 → 10
24 → 9
7 → 22
12 → 21

Pathway

When steps 1 and 2 are completed, reposition the threads as shown.

Reposition	*Reposition*
2 → 1	8 → 7
3 → 2	9 → 8
5 → 6	11 → 12
4 → 5	10 → 11
14 → 13	20 → 19
15 → 14	21 → 20
17 → 18	23 → 24
16 → 17	22 → 23

24-strand Flat Braid · *Chevron Zigzag Design with Five Variations*

SETTING UP

This design was developed from Design 38.

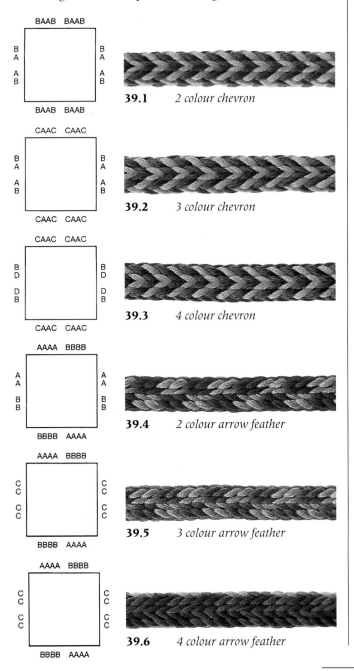

39.1   *2 colour chevron*

39.2   *3 colour chevron*

39.3   *4 colour chevron*

39.4   *2 colour arrow feather*

39.5   *3 colour arrow feather*

39.6   *4 colour arrow feather*

PHOTOGRAPHED SAMPLES

These were made using: 70gm bobbins / 490gm counterbalance / 14 ends 20/2 cotton.

WORKING METHOD

The following making instructions apply to all six patterns.

Maru Dai tension can be controlled either by using 24 bobbins all the same weight with a counterbalance of about 35 per cent of total bobbin weight; or by using 100gm bobbins on the east/west side and 70gm on the north/south side.

Card method tensioning relies on tightening the lower east/west threads before they are moved to their new position.

Note: When cutting the threads allow up to 50 per cent extra in length for the east/west threads.

MARU DAI

To make by Maru Dai, continuously repeat steps 1–6.

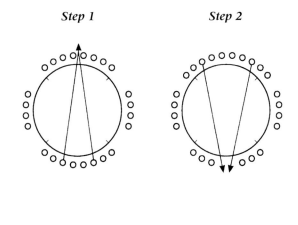

Step 1   *Step 2*

Step 3

Step 4

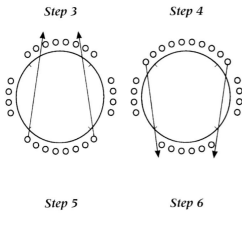

Step 5

Step 6

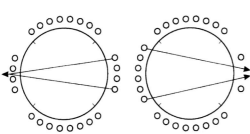

CARD

To make by card, continuously repeat steps 1 and 2.

Home slots   1 2 3 4   7 8 9 10   13 14 17 18   21 22 23 24
27 28 29 30   33 34 37 38

Thread the card, leaving slots empty at 5, 6, 11, 12, 15, 16, 19, 20, 25, 26, 31, 32, 35, 36, 39 and 40.

Step 1

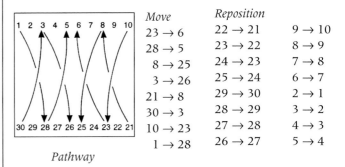

Pathway

Move	Reposition	
23 → 6	22 → 21	9 → 10
28 → 5	23 → 22	8 → 9
8 → 25	24 → 23	7 → 8
3 → 26	25 → 24	6 → 7
21 → 8	29 → 30	2 → 1
30 → 3	28 → 29	3 → 2
10 → 23	27 → 28	4 → 3
1 → 28	26 → 27	5 → 4

Step 2

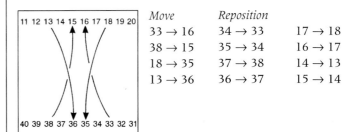

Pathway

Move	Reposition	
33 → 16	34 → 33	17 → 18
38 → 15	35 → 34	16 → 17
18 → 35	37 → 38	14 → 13
13 → 36	36 → 37	15 → 14

24-strand Flat Braid · *Chevron with Two Variations*

SETTING UP

This design was developed from Designs 38 and 39.

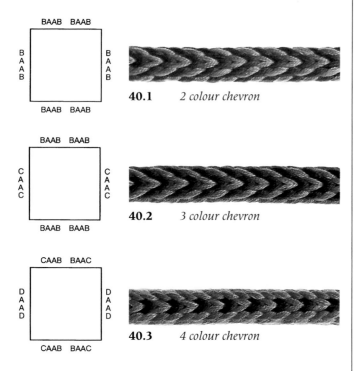

40.1 *2 colour chevron*

40.2 *3 colour chevron*

40.3 *4 colour chevron*

PHOTOGRAPHED SAMPLES

These were made using: 70gm bobbins / 490gm counter-balance / 16 ends 20/2 cotton.

WORKING METHOD

Maru Dai tension can be controlled either by using 24 bobbins all the same weight with a counterbalance of about 35 per cent of total bobbin weight; or by using 100gm bobbins on the east/west side and 70gm on the north/south side.

Card method tensioning relies on tightening the lower east/west threads before they are moved to their new position.

Note: When cutting the threads allow up to 50 per cent extra in length for the east/west threads.

MARU DAI

To make by Maru Dai, continuously repeat steps 1–6.

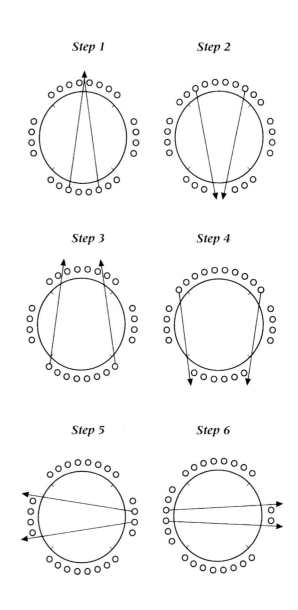

Step 1

Step 2

Step 3

Step 4

Step 5

Step 6

CARD

To make by card, continuously repeat steps 1 and 2.

Home slots   1 2 3 4   7 8 9 10   14 15 16 17   21 22 23 24
27 28 29 30   34 35 36 37

Thread the card, leaving slots empty at 5, 6, 11, 12, 13, 18, 19, 20, 25, 26, 31, 32, 33, 39 and 40.

Step 1

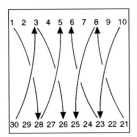

Pathway

Move	Reposition	
23 → 6	22 → 21	9 → 10
28 → 5	23 → 22	8 → 9
8 → 25	24 → 23	7 → 8
3 → 26	25 → 24	6 → 7
21 → 8	29 → 30	2 → 1
30 → 3	28 → 29	3 → 2
10 → 23	27 → 28	4 → 3
1 → 28	26 → 27	5 → 4

Step 2

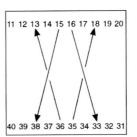

Pathway

Move	Reposition	
35 → 18	37 → 36	14 → 15
36 → 13	38 → 37	13 → 14
15 → 38	34 → 35	17 → 16
16 → 33	33 → 34	18 → 17

20-strand Flat Braid · *Chevron with Three Diamond Variations*

SETTING UP

Patterns 41.2, 41.3 and 41.4 use the same setting-up diagram as 41.1.

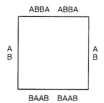

41.1   *2 colour chevron*

41.2   *2 colour small diamond*

41.3   *2 colour small diamond*

41.4   *2 colour small diamond*

PHOTOGRAPHED SAMPLES

These were made using: 70gm bobbins / 490gm counterbalance / 50 ends 200/2 cotton.

WORKING METHOD

To make the four patterns, complete the steps shown below:

Pattern	make steps in this sequence			
41.1	1 2 1 4	repeat		
41.2	1 2 3 4	5 6 7 8	repeat	
41.3	1 2 1 4	3 2 5 8	5 6 7 8	repeat
41.4	1 2 1 4	1 2 3 4	5 6 5 8	5 6 7 8 repeat

Maru Dai tension can be controlled either by using 24 bobbins all the same weight with a counterbalance of about 35 per cent of total bobbin weight; or by using 100gm bobbins on the east/west side and 70gm on the north/south side.

Card method tensioning relies on tightening the lower east/west threads before they are moved to their new position.

Note: When cutting the threads allow up to 75 per cent extra in length for the east/west threads.

MARU DAI

Make to the sequence of steps shown under Working Method. Tighten weft threads after each warp thread movement.

Step 1

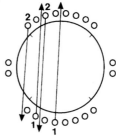
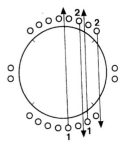

Step 2

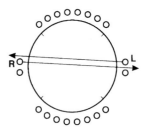

Step 3

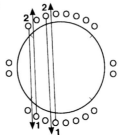
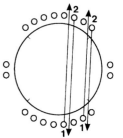

Step 4

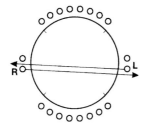

Step 5

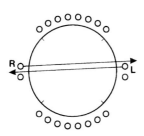

Step 6

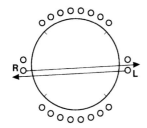

Step 7

Step 8

CARD

Home slots   2 3 4 5 6 7 8 9   15 16   22 23 24 25 26 27 28 29
35 36

Make to the sequence of steps shown under Working
Method.

Step 1

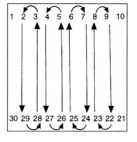

Pathway

Move

2 → 30	9 → 21
3 → 2	8 → 9
28 → 3	23 → 8
4 → 28	7 → 23
5 → 4	6 → 7
26 → 5	25 → 6

Reposition
24 → 25
23 → 24
22 → 23
21 → 22
27 → 26
28 → 27
29 → 28
30 → 29

Step 2

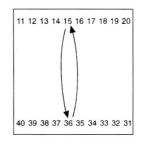

Threads change place

Step 3

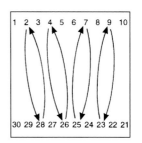

Threads change place

Step 4

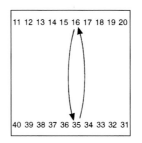

Threads change place

Step 5

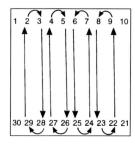

Pathway

Step 6

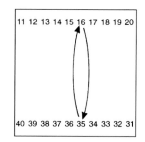

Threads change place

Move

29 → 1	22 → 10
28 → 29	23 → 22
3 → 28	8 → 23
27 → 3	24 → 8
26 → 27	25 → 24
5 → 26	6 → 25

Reposition

4 → 5
3 → 4
2 → 3
1 → 2
7 → 6
8 → 7
9 → 8
10 → 9

Step 7

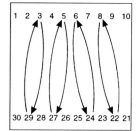

Threads change place

Step 8

Threads change place

16-strand Flat Braid · *Diamond with Five Variations*

SETTING UP

Patterns 42.2, 42.3 and 42.4 use the same setting-up diagram as 42.1.

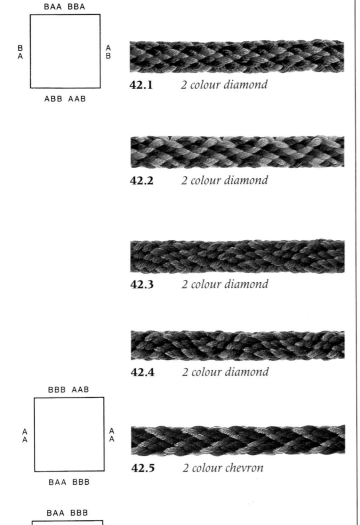

BAA BBA

B   A
A   B

ABB AAB

42.1   *2 colour diamond*

42.2   *2 colour diamond*

42.3   *2 colour diamond*

42.4   *2 colour diamond*

BBB AAB

A   A
A   A

BAA BBB

42.5   *2 colour chevron*

BAA BBB

A   A
A   A

BBB AAB

42.6   *2 colour diamond*

PHOTOGRAPHED SAMPLES

These were made using: 70gm bobbins / 490gm counter-balance / 15 ends 20/2 cotton.

WORKING METHOD

To make all six patterns, complete the steps shown below.

Pattern	make steps in this sequence
42.1	1 2 3 4 5 6 7 8 repeat
42.2	1 2 1 2 3 4 5 6 5 6 7 8 repeat
42.3	1 2 1 2 1 2 3 4 5 6 5 6 5 6 7 8 repeat
42.4	1 2 1 2 1 2 1 2 3 4 5 6 5 6 5 6 5 6 7 8 repeat
42.5	1 6 3 8 5 2 7 4 repeat
42.6	1 6 3 8 5 2 7 4 repeat

Maru Dai tension can be controlled either by using 24 bobbins all the same weight with a counterbalance of about 45 per cent of total bobbin weight; or by using 100gm bobbins on the east/west side and 70gm on the north/south side.

Card method tensioning relies on tightening the lower east/west threads before they are moved to their new position.

Note: When cutting the threads allow up to 75 per cent extra in length for the east/west threads.

MARU DAI

Make to the sequence of steps shown under Working Method. Tighten weft threads after each warp thread movement.

Step 1

Step 5

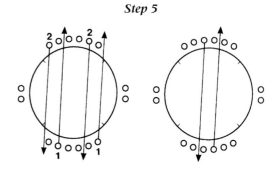

Step 2

Step 6

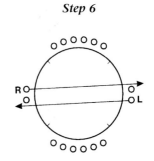

Step 3

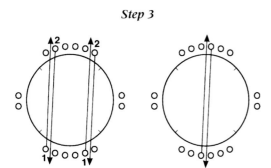

Step 7

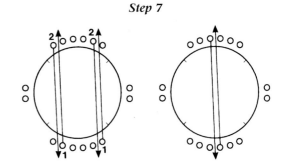

Step 4

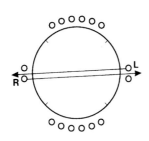

Step 8

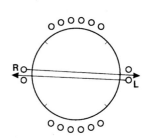

CARD

Home slots   3 4 5 6 7 8   15 16   23 24 25 26 27 28   35 36

Make to the sequence of steps shown under Working Method.

Step 1

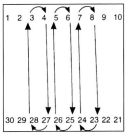

Pathway

Move	Reposition
8 → 22	
7 → 8	27 → 28
24 → 7	26 → 27
6 → 24	25 → 26
5 → 6	24 → 25
26 → 5	23 → 24
4 → 26	22 → 23
3 → 4	
28 → 3	

Step 2

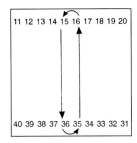

Pathway

Move
15 → 37
16 → 15
35 → 16
36 → 35
37 → 36

Step 3

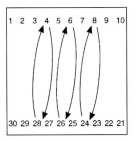

Threads change place

Step 4

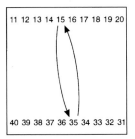

Threads change place

Step 5

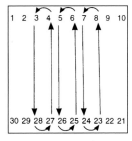

Pathway

Move	Reposition
3 → 29	24 → 23
4 → 3	25 → 24
27 → 4	26 → 25
5 → 27	27 → 26
6 → 5	28 → 27
25 → 6	29 → 28
7 → 25	
8 → 7	
23 → 8	

Step 6

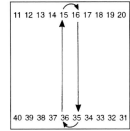

Pathway

Move
16 → 34
15 → 16
36 → 15
35 → 36
34 → 35

Step 7

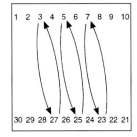

Threads change place

Step 8

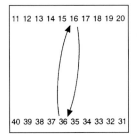

Threads change place

16-strand Flat Braid · *Small Diamond Design*

SETTING UP

The Peruvian braid on which this design is based used A threads that were thicker than B threads, which gave a pleasing result. The braid also stands up well when the A and B threads are the same thickness. A stained-glass window effect can be achieved by using multicoloured A threads.

43.1   *2 colour*

PHOTOGRAPHED SAMPLE

This was made using: 70gm bobbins / 490gm counterbalance / 15 ends 20/2 cotton.

WORKING METHOD

Maru Dai tension can be controlled either by using bobbins all the same weight with a counterbalance of about 45 per cent of total bobbin weight; or by using 100gm bobbins on the east/west side and 70gm on the north/south side.

Card method tensioning relies on tightening the lower east/west threads before they are moved to their new position.

Note: When cutting the threads allow up to 50 per cent extra in length for the east/west threads.

MARU DAI

To make by Maru Dai, continuously repeat steps 1 to 8. Tighten weft threads after each warp thread movement.

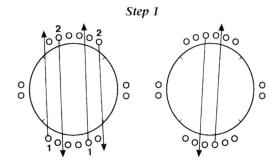

Step 1

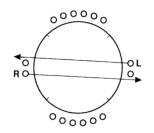

Step 2

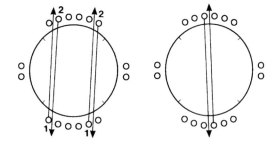

Step 3

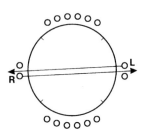

Step 4

Step 5

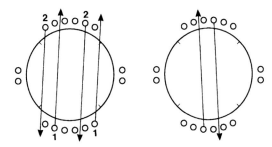

Step 6

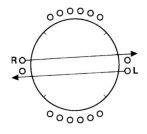

Step 7

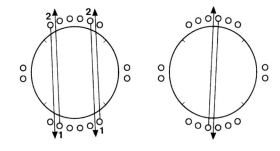

Step 8

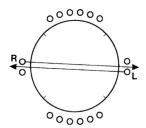

CARD

Home slots   3 4 5 6 7 8   15 16   23 24 25 26 27 28   35 36
  To make by card, continuously repeat steps 1–8.

Step 1

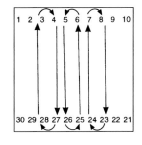

Pathway

Move

8 → 22	28 → 2
7 → 8	27 → 28
24 → 7	4 → 27
23 → 24	3 → 4
22 → 23	2 → 3
5 → 29	
6 → 5	
25 → 6	
26 → 25	
29 → 26	

Step 2

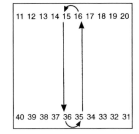

Pathway

Move

15 → 37
16 → 15
35 → 16
36 → 35
37 → 36

Step 3

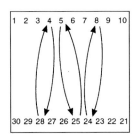

Threads change place

Step 4

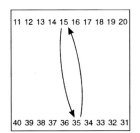

Threads change place

Step 5

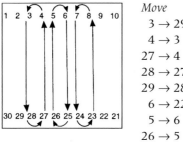

Pathway

Move

3 → 29	23 → 9
4 → 3	24 → 23
27 → 4	7 → 24
28 → 27	8 → 7
29 → 28	9 → 8
6 → 22	
5 → 6	
26 → 5	
25 → 26	
22 → 25	

Step 7

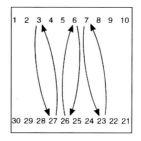

Threads change place

Step 6

Pathway

Move

16 → 34
15 → 16
36 → 15
35 → 36
34 → 35

Step 8

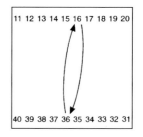

Threads change place

Opposite   This adjustable wrist piece, made from Design 46, was worked in one end of silk to each bobbin. The beads were threaded on during braiding.

Spiral Braids

The structure of Designs 45 and 48 is known in Japan as Kongo, which means hard like a diamond. Not all the patterns shown in this section are of Japanese origin, some were discovered by enquiring students – Design 46, for example, was developed out of curiosity and arose from the question, 'What would happen if the threads were arranged like this?' There are many more possible combinations than have been shown, and further patterns can be produced by using more than two colours and by adding texture.

Design 47 was discovered by a student who took Design 46 a stage further. The core gives the ridge a much firmer finish. Piping cord or something similar could be used as the core, but whatever you use must be the same colour as the active threads.

Design 48 shows how to reverse the spiral; the method is similar to that used to work Design 26.

The card used to make these spiral braids is a circular, un-numbered card with 32 slots (see Fig. 17c). It is not necessary to number the slots in the card as the moves for the card are identical to the Maru Dai diagrams.

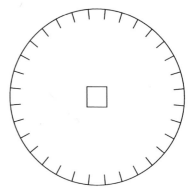

Fig. 17c

44

WORLDWIDE

8-strand Spiral with One Variation

SETTING UP

Instructions to change the direction of the spiral are given in Design 48.

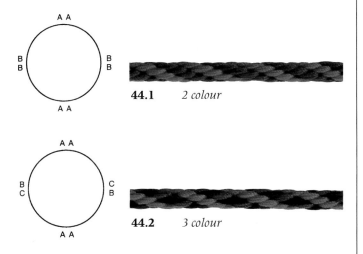

44.1   *2 colour*

44.2   *3 colour*

PHOTOGRAPHED SAMPLES

These were made using: 100gm bobbins / 600gm counterbalance / 8 ends 30/3 silk.

WORKING METHOD

Diagrams for the card method are the same as the Maru Dai shown below. To make, continuously repeat steps 1 and 2.

MARU DAI AND CARD

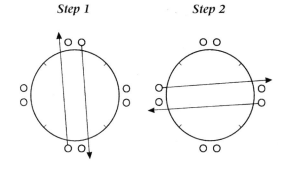

Step 1   *Step 2*

45

16-strand Spiral with 11 Variations

SETTING UP

New patterns can be made by experimenting with the setting-up patterns and arranging colours in different ways. To reverse the spiral, follow the instructions shown in Design 48.

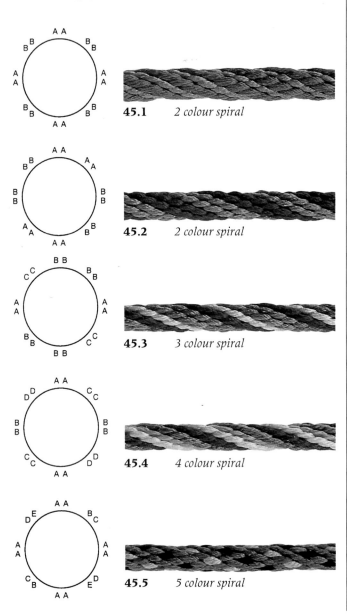

45.1 *2 colour spiral*

45.2 *2 colour spiral*

45.3 *3 colour spiral*

45.4 *4 colour spiral*

45.5 *5 colour spiral*

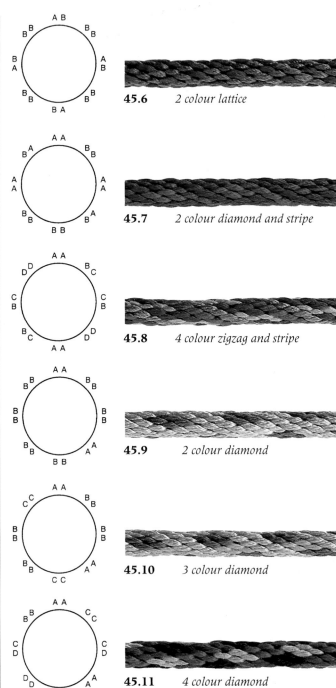

45.6 *2 colour lattice*

45.7 *2 colour diamond and stripe*

45.8 *4 colour zigzag and stripe*

45.9 *2 colour diamond*

45.10 *3 colour diamond*

45.11 *4 colour diamond*

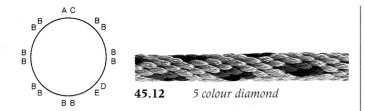

45.12   *5 colour diamond*

MARU DAI AND CARD

PHOTOGRAPHED SAMPLES

These were made using: 100gm bobbins / 650gm counter-balance / 5 ends 20/3 silk.

WORKING METHOD

Diagrams for the card method are the same as the Maru Dai shown below. When making patterns 45.9–45.12 check the beginning of the braid to see if a well-defined pattern is being made. These patterns sometimes slip and make an elongated shape instead of diamonds, and if this happens, undo the work and try restarting the braid on the east/west side (start with step 3).

To make, continuously repeat steps 1–4.

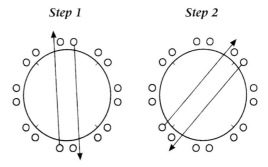

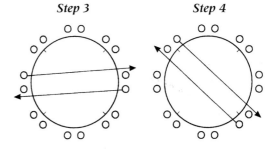

Ridged Spiral with Nine Variations

SETTING UP

These patterns can be made by the card method only when all the threads are the same thickness, and care must be taken to pull firmly on the B threads.

Set up the braid with bobbins of the same weight and with threads of the same thickness.

Changes to the angle of spiral and height of the ridge can be made either by increasing the weight of B thread bobbins, or by increasing the thickness of A threads. If required, additional colours can be introduced to both A and B bobbins.

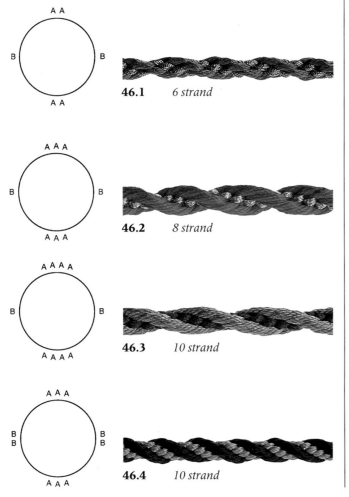

46.1   *6 strand*

46.2   *8 strand*

46.3   *10 strand*

46.4   *10 strand*

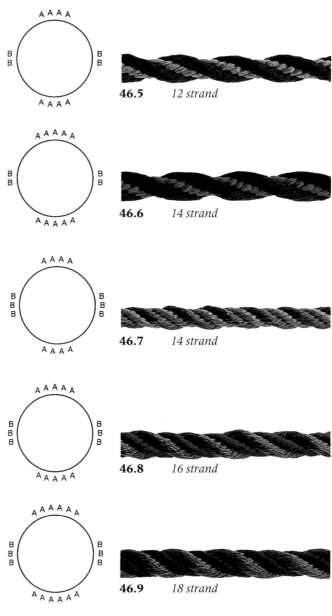

46.5   *12 strand*

46.6   *14 strand*

46.7   *14 strand*

46.8   *16 strand*

46.9   *18 strand*

PHOTOGRAPHED SAMPLES

These were made using: 100gm bobbins / various counter-balance / various ends 20/3 silk.

WORKING METHOD

Diagrams for the card method are the same as the Maru Dai shown below. When crossing the B threads over the centre hole of the Maru Dai, gently lift the bobbins that are under tension. This will help to form the ridge so that it stands high from the A threads.

The two steps shown illustrate the movement of the threads for pattern 46.5 All the patterns follow these two steps, with the outer threads moving in a clockwise direction, regardless of the number of threads in the pattern.

To make, continuously repeat steps 1 and 2.

MARU DAI AND CARD

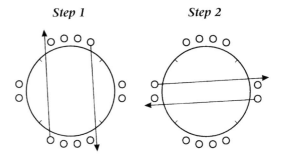

Step 1 *Step 2*

47

Ridged Spiral with Core

SETTING UP

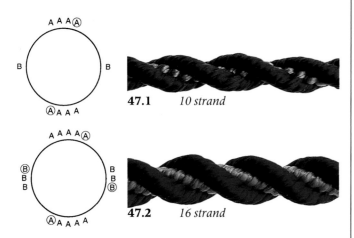

47.1 *10 strand*

47.2 *16 strand*

Ⓐ and Ⓑ show the position of the core threads.

Two examples are shown to illustrate the principle of working with a core, which gives a much firmer and higher finish. The core method can be applied to all the patterns shown in Design 46. This design is not suitable for the card method.

PHOTOGRAPHED SAMPLES

Pattern 47.1 was made using: A – 100gm bobbins / B – 150gm bobbins / 540gm counterbalance / 3 ends lyra silk / 9 ends core.

WORKING METHOD

The movements that make core braids are the same as for the previous designs, with one exception – the core never moves, but remains passive throughout the whole length of the braid.

Before they complete the normal spiral movement, the active bobbins are taken under the core bobbins, wrapping around and hiding the core thread. The core thread should be the same colour as the A or B threads. The thickness of

the core thread works well when it is between three and five times thicker than the active threads.

To make, continuously repeat steps 1 and 2.

MARU DAI

Pattern 47.1

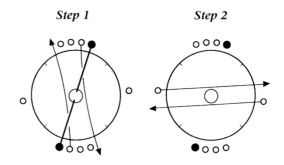

Step 1   **Step 2**

● shows the core bobbins in position.

Pattern 47.2

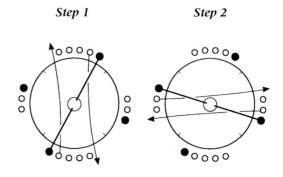

Step 1   **Step 2**

48

Reversing the Spiral

SETTING UP

This design is created by reversing the spiral for Designs 44, 45 and 46. The set-up patterns for these designs should be used.

PHOTOGRAPHED SAMPLE

This was made using: 100gm bobbins / 950gm counter-balance / 5 ends 20/3 silk.

WORKING METHOD

Reversing the spiral after a given number of moves allows the braider to make a zigzag pattern along the length of the braid. To begin, try a count of 24, then change direction, then count 24 in the opposite direction and change again. A count of one is when two threads from the opposing pairs move (as in step 1). A count of 8 or 12 or 16 can also be used.

MARU DAI

To reverse the spiral from a clockwise-turning Z spiral to an anticlockwise-turning S spiral, follow the instructions below.

1 Before changing, align the last group of threads worked on a north/south axis.

2 Lift all upper threads on the right-hand side over the lower threads on the left-hand side (Fig. 43).

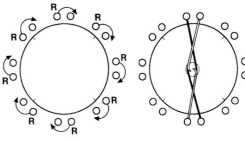

Fig. 43

3 Begin to work in an anticlockwise direction (see steps 1–4 below), starting with the group of threads that lie to the right-hand side of the last worked pair.

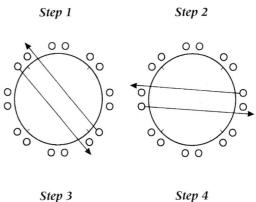

Step 1 *Step 2*

Step 3 *Step 4*

4 Before changing back to the clockwise-turning movement, align the last group of threads worked on a north/south axis.

5 Lift all upper threads on the left-hand side over the lower threads on the right-hand side (Fig. 44).

6 Begin to work in a clockwise direction, starting with the group of threads that lie to the left-hand side of the last worked pair (as in Design 45, steps 1–4).

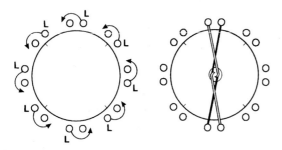

Fig. 44

CARD

1 Before reversing the spiral on the card, finish the sequence of moves so that two empty slots are left between each colour group.

2 Follow the instructions shown above for the Maru Dai, lifting the right-hand upper threads over the left-hand lower threads into the next empty slot.

3 Work the braid so that the card turns in a clockwise direction as the threads move in an anticlockwise direction.

4 To change back, finish the sequence of moves so that two empty slots are left between each colour group.

5 Lift the left-hand upper threads over the right-hand lower threads into the next empty slot.

6 Work the braid so that the card turns in an anticlockwise direction as the threads move clockwise.

Opposite   *A hollow braid, worked in Design 49, was made around a hairband using 3mm polyester ribbon. Flowers and beads were added to the tassels.*

Hollow and 3-, 5- and 6-sided Braids

This last section shows how to make designs that are round and hollow, and it introduces 3-, 5- and 6-sided braids. Design 49 is a hollow braid that has a direct association with Mediterranean countries, with its origin in Celtic cultures. This tubular, interlaced structure has many applications as a basketry technique – fish traps are one such use. Design 49 is a braid known in Japan, and Design 50 is seen as a development of Design 49. Both designs can be made around a core to maintain permanent lacy hollow tubes.

There are 40 seafaring braids, known as solid sinnets, in *The Ashley Book of Knots*, all of which can be made on the Maru Dai in a two-handed movement, regardless of whether there is an odd or even number of threads. Five of these designs are shown in this section: Designs 51, 52, 54, 55 and 56 are Ashley's design numbers 3043, 3047, 3052, 3080 and 3081 respectively. These designs should enable other braids to be worked out by the inquisitive braider.

Ashley's book includes an illustration of a three-legged stool; a device used to make solid sinnets.

The last design in the book is for a 31-strand pentalpha braid, and if you can master this one, try the 61-strand pentalpha braid – you will need a 290mm (11½in) diameter card cut with 120 slots!

CARD METHOD

Designs 49–55 use a round card with 48 slots. The card for Design 56 has 80 slots. Details of the cards are given in Figs. 17d and 17e.

The card has been designed with number 1 to the west side. As with the circular card for Designs 44–48, it can be rotated to accommodate the moves to be made.

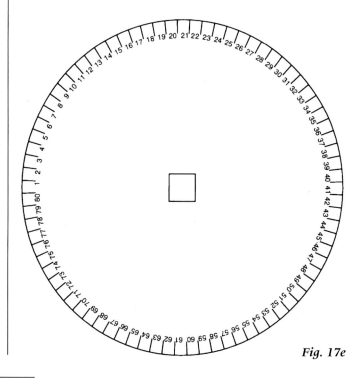

Fig. 17d

Fig. 17e

16-strand Hollow Braid · *Spiral with Three Variations*

SETTING UP

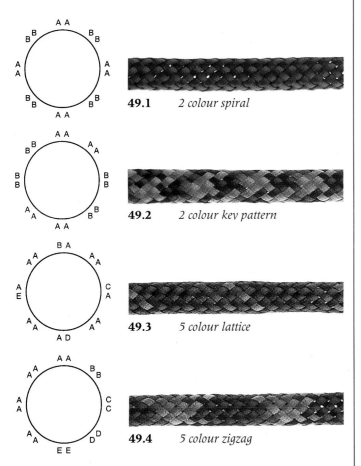

49.1 *2 colour spiral*

49.2 *2 colour key pattern*

49.3 *5 colour lattice*

49.4 *5 colour zigzag*

PHOTOGRAPHED SAMPLES

These were made using: 70gm bobbins / 660gm counter-balance / core 10mm (⅜in) dowel stick / Offray ribbon.

WORKING METHOD

The movements that make this braid may be familiar to many people as the Grand Dance in maypole dancing. The structure is also frequently used in industry to make tubular coverings for tassels, electrical cables and ropes.

This design can also be made with 12, 24 or 32 strands.

MARU DAI

To make by Maru Dai, continuously repeat steps 1–8. To keep the braid hollow throughout its length, make around a core (see Design 11 for details).

Step 1   *Step 2*

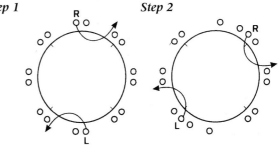

Step 3   *Step 4*

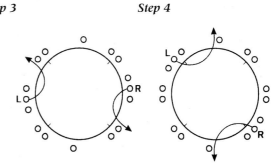

Step 5   *Step 6*

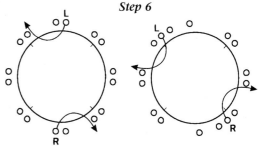

Step 7 **Step 8**

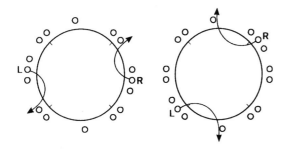

Home slots   2 3 8 9   14 15 20 21   26 27 32 33   38 39 44 45

To make by card, continuously repeat steps 1–2.

Step 1	Step 2	*Reposition*
14 → 19	15 → 10	19 → 20
20 → 25	9 → 4	22 → 21
26 → 31	3 → 46	25 → 26
32 → 37	45 → 40	28 → 27
38 → 43	39 → 34	31 → 32
44 → 1	33 → 28	34 → 33
2 → 7	27 → 22	37 → 38
8 → 14	21 → 15	40 → 39
		43 → 44
		46 → 45
		1 → 2
		4 → 3
		7 → 8
		10 → 9

50

16-strand Hollow Braid · *Vertical Stripe with Seven Variations*

SETTING UP

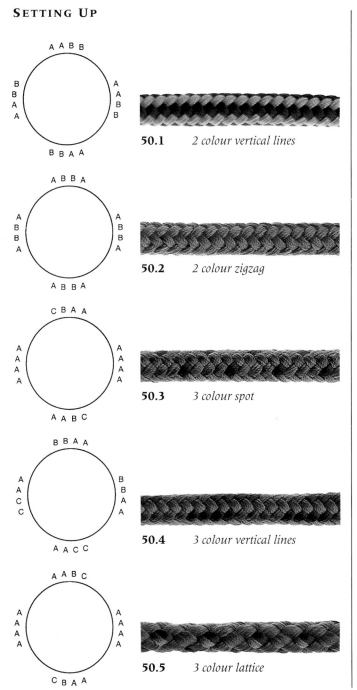

50.1   *2 colour vertical lines*

50.2   *2 colour zigzag*

50.3   *3 colour spot*

50.4   *3 colour vertical lines*

50.5   *3 colour lattice*

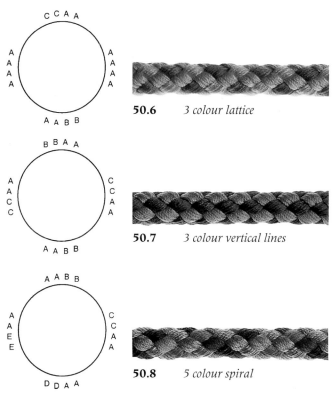

50.6   *3 colour lattice*

50.7   *3 colour vertical lines*

50.8   *5 colour spiral*

PHOTOGRAPHED SAMPLES

These were made using: 70gm bobbins / 660gm counter-balance / core 6mm (¼in) dowel stick / 9 ends 30/3 silk.

WORKING METHOD

To make the three patterns, complete the steps shown below.

Pattern	make steps in this sequence
50.1–50.4	1 2 3 4
50.5–50.8	1 2 1 2 3 4 3 4

MARU DAI

Make to the sequence of steps shown under Working Method. To keep the braid hollow throughout its length make around a core.

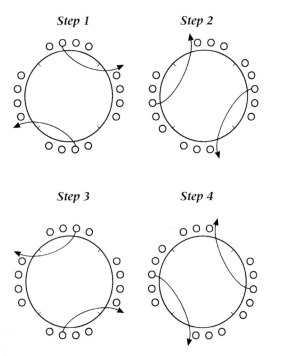

Step 1   **Step 2**

Step 3   **Step 4**

CARD

Home slots   1 2 3 4   13 14 15 16   25 26 27 28   37 38 39 40

Make to the sequence of steps shown under Working Method.

Step 1	**Step 2**	*Reposition*
14 → 24	26 → 36	13 → 14
38 → 48	2 → 12	12 → 13
		25 → 26
		24 → 25
		37 → 38
		36 → 37
		1 → 2
		48 → 1

Step 3	**Step 4**	*Reposition*
15 → 5	27 → 17	16 → 15
39 → 29	3 → 41	17 → 16
		28 → 27
		29 → 28
		40 → 39
		41 → 40
		4 → 3
		5 → 4

51

SEAFARING

11-strand Triangular Braid · *Two-colour with One Variation*

SETTING UP

The setting-up diagrams show the bobbin positions for the Maru Dai and the home slots for the card method.

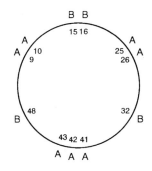

51.1   *2 colour*

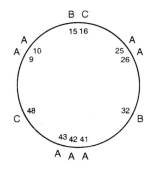

51.2   *3 colour*

PHOTOGRAPHED SAMPLES

These were made using: 70gm bobbins / 380gm counter-balance / 9 ends 30/3 silk.

WORKING METHOD

To make, continuously repeat steps 1–3.

MARU DAI

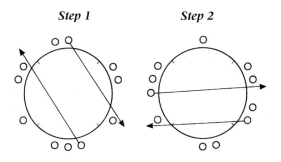

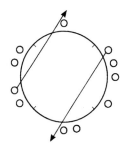

CARD

Home slots: see setting-up diagram.

Step 1	Step 2	Step 3
41 → 11	9 → 27	25 → 43
42 → 41	10 → 9	26 → 25
43 → 42	11 → 10	27 → 26
16 → 31	32 → 47	48 → 15
15 → 16	31 → 32	47 → 48

19-strand Triangular Braid

SETTING UP

The setting-up diagram shows the bobbin positions for the Maru Dai and the home slots for the card method. When preparing the warp, cut the A threads 30 per cent longer, because these threads work harder than the B and C threads.

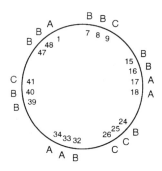

3 colours

PHOTOGRAPHED SAMPLE

This was made using: 70gm bobbins / 660gm counterbalance / 9 ends 30/3 silk.

WORKING METHOD

To make, continuously repeat steps 1–6.

MARU DAI

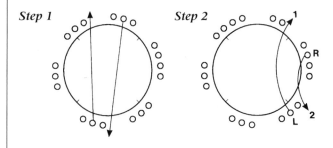

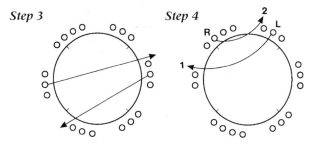

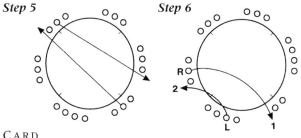

CARD

Home slots: see setting-up diagram.

Step 1	Step 2	Step 3
33 → 2	25 → 10	17 → 34
34 → 33	26 → 25	18 → 17
8 → 31	16 → 23	40 → 15
7 → 8	15 → 16	39 → 40

Step 4	Step 5	Step 6
9 → 42	1 → 18	41 → 26
10 → 9	2 → 1	42 → 41
48 → 7	24 → 47	32 → 39
47 → 48	23 → 24	31 → 32

18-strand Triangular Braid · *Two-colour Vertical Stripe with Three Variations*

SETTING UP

The setting-up diagrams show the bobbin positions for the Maru Dai and the home slots for the card method.

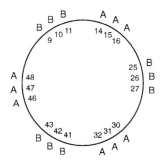

53.1 *2 colour*

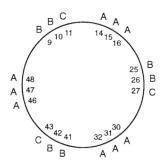

53.2 *3 colour*

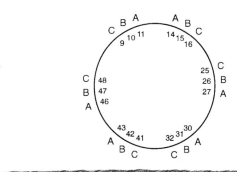

53.3 *3 colour*

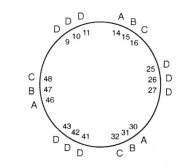

53.4 *4 colour*

PHOTOGRAPHED SAMPLES

These were made using: 70gm bobbins / 840gm counter-balance / 15 ends 20/2 cotton.

WORKING METHOD

To make by Maru Dai, continuously repeat steps 1–3.

MARU DAI

Step 1

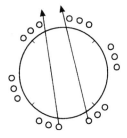

Step 2

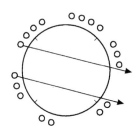

Step 3

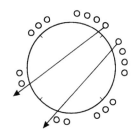

CARD

Home slots: see setting-up diagram.
    To make by card, continuously repeat steps 1–6.

Step 1	Step 2	Step 3
41 → 12	9 → 28	16 → 45
32 → 13	48 → 29	25 → 44

Step 4	Step 5	Step 6
10 → 9	26 → 25	42 → 41
11 → 10	27 → 26	43 → 42
12 → 11	28 → 27	44 → 43
15 → 16	31 → 32	47 → 48
14 → 15	30 → 31	46 → 47
13 → 14	29 → 30	45 → 46

20-strand Hexagonal Braid · *Three-colour with Two Variations*

SETTING UP

The setting-up diagrams show the bobbin positions for the Maru Dai and the home slots for the card method.

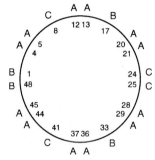

54.1   *3 colour*

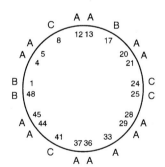

54.2   *3 colour*

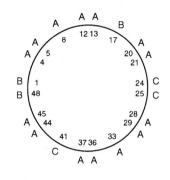

54.3   *3 colour*

PHOTOGRAPHED SAMPLES

These were made using: 70gm bobbins / 800gm counter-balance / 2 ends knitting silk.

WORKING METHOD

To make by Maru Dai, continuously repeat steps 1–6.

MARU DAI

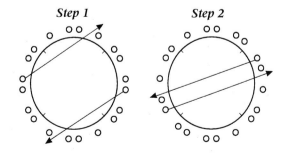

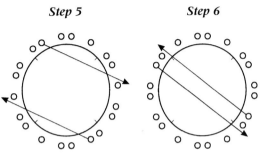

Step 3   *Step 4*

Step 5   *Step 6*

CARD

Home slots: see setting-up diagram.

Step 1	Step 2	Step 3
1 → 16	20 → 46	41 → 7
48 → 1	21 → 20	40 → 41
25 → 40	44 → 21	17 → 32
24 → 25	45 → 44	16 → 17
	46 → 45	

Step 4	Step 5	Step 6
36 → 14	8 → 24	28 → 6
37 → 36	7 → 8	29 → 28
12 → 37	33 → 48	4 → 29
13 → 12	32 → 33	5 → 4
14 → 13		6 → 5

16-strand Pentagon Braid · *Two-colour with One Variation*

SETTING UP

The setting-up diagrams show the bobbin positions for the Maru Dai and the home slots for the card method.

When preparing the threads, cut the A threads 30 per cent longer because these threads work harder than the B and C threads.

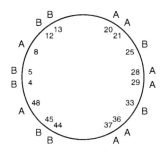

55.1   *2 colour*

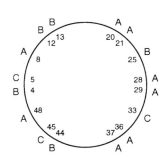

55.2   *3 colour*

PHOTOGRAPHED SAMPLES

These were made using: 70gm bobbins / 660gm counter-balance / 9 ends 30/3 silk.

WORKING METHOD

To make, continuously repeat steps 1–5.

MARU DAI

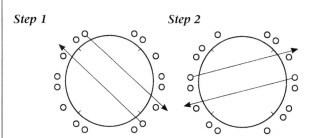

Step 1   *Step 2*

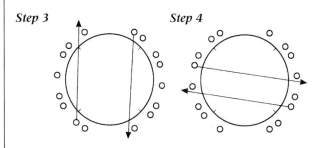

Step 3   *Step 4*

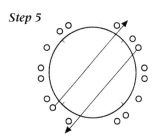

Step 5

CARD

Home slots: see setting-up diagram.

Step 1	Step 2	Step 3
36 → 9	28 → 1	45 → 12
37 → 36	29 → 28	44 → 45
13 → 32	5 → 24	20 → 37
12 → 13	4 → 5	21 → 20

Step 4	Step 5
33 → 4	25 → 44
32 → 33	24 → 25
8 → 29	48 → 21
9 → 8	1 → 48

31-strand Pentalpha Braid

SETTING UP

For this design a card 230mm (9in) in diameter will be required; mark and cut 80 slots.

The setting-up diagrams show the bobbin positions for the Maru Dai and the home slots for the card method.

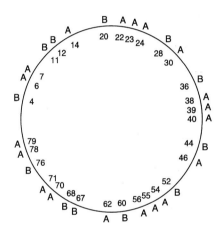

2 colour

PHOTOGRAPHED SAMPLE

This was made using: 83.5gm bobbins / 1310gm counter-balance / 3 ends 20/3 silk.

WORKING METHOD

The braid can be worked on the Maru Dai by those braiders who have 31 bobbins. The method of working on the Maru Dai can be planned by studying the card method.

To make, continuously repeat steps 1–5.

CARD

Home slots: see setting-up diagram.

Step 1	Step 2	Step 3
68 → 75	52 → 59	36 → 43
67 → 68	51 → 52	35 → 36
78 → 63	62 → 47	46 → 31
79 → 78	63 → 62	47 → 46
54 → 8	38 → 72	22 → 56
55 → 54	39 → 38	23 → 22
56 → 55	40 → 39	24 → 23
12 → 51	76 → 35	60 → 19
11 → 12	75 → 76	59 → 60

Step 4	Step 5
20 → 27	4 → 11
19 → 20	3 → 4
30 → 15	14 → 79
31 → 30	15 → 14
6 → 40	70 → 24
7 → 6	71 → 70
8 → 7	72 → 71
44 → 3	28 → 67
43 → 44	27 → 28

Appendix

Mathematics and Braids

It is only in the last few years that I have become aware that in working with braids I work with mathematics. I had never thought about it until Anne Watson, Head of Mathematics at Peers School, Oxford, took a cardboard device and worked Design 18 with a group of students. This led to an in-service course for teachers, and the idea was later introduced to the Association of Teachers of Mathematics at their annual conference.

It is hoped that by including this section on mathematics and braids, other teachers will see the value for both textile and mathematics projects. The design that appears on the surface of the braid is created by arranging coloured threads in a certain order. A repeating pattern will be made by moving them from point to point in a series of steps along a predetermined pathway. Designs can be changed either by altering the colour arrangement when setting up or by varying the sequence of steps in the pathway. The designs can also be extended by increasing the number of threads used, thereby increasing the complexity of the pathway.

In this book six different card devices are used to make braids, each with its own system of notation. The notation describes points on the cards that threads move from and to, and therefore provides a starting place for mathematical analysis.

SOME POSSIBLE MATHEMATICAL APPLICATIONS

Arithmetic

Before a braid can be made, a card has to be measured, cut and numbered. The thread has to be chosen, cut to length, allowing for loss of length in the making, and a series of rules, with do's and don'ts, has to be followed.

Pattern

The instructions to make any particular design mean that a series of steps is followed that will eventually bring all the threads back to their original starting place. Braids, therefore, have an underlying closed structure that lends itself to mathematical inquiry, and they are, in fact, related to certain kinds of abstract groups, which are sometimes studied in higher mathematics.

In addition, there are a variety of other aspects which can lead to mathematical questions:

* What two-dimensional shapes are made; does the braid form a square, a rectangle, a circle, a triangle or a pentagon?
* Is the structure symmetrical?
* Can the braid be made by turning the card through 90°, thereby making it rotationally symmetrical?

Graph Theory

Graph theory is not about drawing graphs. It is about drawing networks, tracing the pathway of one particular thread along its journey, which would enable all the threads to be compared to see if they all follow the same pathway. It is about establishing how many movements are needed for any particular thread to arrive back at its original starting place. Graph theory is also concerned with questions such as 'How many ways would there be of visiting certain points?' 'What is the longest route?' 'What is the shortest route?' The answers to these questions would enable different braids to be designed.

Maypole dances make braids around a pole by following a pathway. Country dances can also be made into braids, the dancer becoming the thread. Likewise braids, can become country dances.

When the Grand Dance around the maypole is performed, a hollow, interlaced braid is made. When the ribbon length is exhausted, the dancers turn the opposite way and dance to undo the braid, inverting the structure. Inverse structures are also found in solid and flat braids, in particular in the diamond designs from Peru and Japan. The idea of 'doing and undoing' and using inverses is central in many branches of mathematics.

Bell-ringing sequences can be made into braids, each bell represented by a different colour, allowing the pathway for each bell to be traced.

CONSTRAINTS

There are several constraints to be considered when using a cardboard device:

* Each card has a certain number of slots
* Certain moves can be made
* Clockwise and anticlockwise movements are possible
* The colour and thickness of the threads will affect the result.

More is learnt by changing the smallest thing than by changing lots of things at once. The small change can be traced and recorded. Changing things systematically could eventually lead to a better understanding of the whole structure. By exploring braids in this way people are using the same techniques that professional mathematicians and scientists use. This could be applied, for example, to a sequence of steps: what would happen if the sequence was interrupted? For example, if the basic sequence is 1 2 3 4 5 6 7 8, what would happen if two new steps were introduced – 1 2 1 2 3 4 5 6 7 8? The path of a single thread through a braid could be more easily traced if the colour of that thread were colour A, while the rest of the threads were all colour B.

EVERYDAY ACTIVITY

Braid-makers and, of course, other textile workers are not consciously aware of how much mathematics they use from the start of a project to its completion.

Here is a list of mathematical activities taken from *The Early Years Mathematics* published by Harcourt Brace Jovanovich, London. The activities listed correspond closely to parts of the National Curriculum, and all of these aspects can be applied to the braids in this book.

Handling data
Matching, comparing, recording and classifying.

Using and applying information
Estimating, questioning, memorizing, predicting, observing, testing, selecting, problem-solving and explaining.

Shapes and space
Pattern-making, angles, spatial awareness, position, construction, symmetry, two-dimensional shapes, rotation, enlargement and reflection.

Measures
Length, ratio, weight, density, horizontal, vertical and time.

Numbers
Counting and computation.

Algebra
Copying, number sequence and pattern, odd, even, pattern recognition, representing, repeating co-ordinates, double and half symbols.

Further Reading

KUMIHIMO BRAIDING

English Texts

Dusenberry, Mary, 'Braiding in Japan' in *Celebration of the Curious Mind*, Interweave Press Inc., USA, 1983

Kinoshita, Masako, two articles on 'Kumihimo', Shuttle, Spindle & Dyepot, USA, 1977 and 1980

Kinoshita, Masako, A braiding technique documented in an early 19th-century Japanese treatise, 'Soshun Biko', The Textile Museum Journal, USA, 1986

Kliot, Kaethe and Jules, *Kumihimo*, Kliot, USA, 1977

Martin, Catherine, *Kumihimo*, Old Hall Press, UK, 1986

Sahashi, Kei (editor), *Exquisite: The World of Japanese Kumihimo Braiding*, Kodansha, London, UK, 1988

Shima, Yukiko, *A Step to Kimono and Kumihimo* (edited by Kyoto Kimono Gakuin), Japan, 1979

Speiser, Noemi, *The Art of Japanese Braiding*, CIBA Geigy Review, Basel, Switzerland, 1974

Speiser, Noemi, *The Manual of Braiding*, Speiser, Basel, Switzerland, 1983

Tada, Makiko, *Kumihimo*, Japanese Festival Office, Washington Arts Centre, Tyne & Wear, UK, 1984

Tokoro, Hoko, *Kumihimo in Japan*, Ogaki Unesco Association, Japan, 1983

Japanese Texts

Domyo, Shimbie, *The Evolution of Kogei Kumihimo* (written in French), Ceita Bulletin no. 24, 1966

Fujita, Shozaburo, *Designing Kumihimo*, Bijutsu Shuppan-Sha, Tokyo, Japan, 1981

Fujita, Shozaburo, article on 'Temple Braids', Nagomi Kumihimo (special issue, no. 6), Tokyo, Japan, 1984

Harano, Mitsuko, *Traditional Kumihimo*, Nakosha, Tokyo, Japan, 1976

Harano, Mitsuko, *Kumihimo of Kaku Dai*, Nippon Vogue, Tokyo, Japan, 1979

Heiro, Kita Gawa and Jusuke, Fukami, *Kara Kumi Dai*, National Treasures Series, Kodansha, Tokyo, Japan

Hirata, Tamaki, *The Works of Tamaki Hirata* vol. 1, Tamaki Hirata, Tokyo, Japan, 1985

Hirata, Tamaki, *The Works of Tamaki Hirata* vol. 2, Tamaki Hirata, Tokyo, Japan, 1990

Iwata, Junichiro, *Traditions of Kumihimo*, private letters, Japan, 1986

Matsushita, Hoetsu, *Kumihimo: An Original Work (Taka Dai)*, Hirai Kiho, Iga Ueno, Japan, 1983

Miura, Yoyai, *The Design of Korai Kumihimo* vol. 1, Miura Yoyai, Japan, 1986

Miura, Yoyai, *The Design of Korai Kumihimo* vol. 2, Miura Yoyai, Japan, 1988

Miura, Yoyai, *Korai Kumihimo*, four specialist booklets, Miura Yoyai, Japan, 1990

Murasugi, Kunio, *The Geometry of Kumihimo*, Kodansha, Tokyo, Japan, 1982

Nagamuma, Shizuka, *Beautiful Kumihimo* vol. 1, Tairyusha, Tokyo, Japan, 1977

Nagamuma, Shizuka, *Beautiful Kumihimo* vol. 2, Tairyusha, Tokyo, Japan, 1977

Nakayama, Aya, *Kumihimo Jewellery*, Bijutsu Shuppan-Sha, Tokyo, Japan, 1979

Okamura, Kayo, *Colour Examples of Kumihimo*, Nippon Vogue, Tokyo, Japan, 1979

Okamura, Kayo, *Kumihimo*, Shafu To Sevkatsu-Sha, Japan, 1976

Ota, Tosaburo, Suganuma, Kojiro and Yamaki, Kaoru, *Kumihimo of Otsu*, Minzokubunka Kenkyukai, Kyoto, Japan, 1969

Sakai, Aiko, *Kumihimo* vol. 1, Nippon Vogue, Tokyo, Japan, 1978

Sakai, Aiko, *Kumihimo* vol. 2, Nippon Vogue, Tokyo, Japan, 1985

Sakai, Aiko, *Kumihimo* vol. 3, Nippon Vogue, Tokyo, Japan, 1990

Sakai, Aiko and Tada, Makiko, *Kumihimo: Advanced Aya Taka Dai*, Sohbi Braiding Association, Tokyo, Japan, 1983

Shoisoin Office, *Shosoin No Kumihimo*, Heibonsha, Japan, 1973

Shufuno, Tomosha and Yamaoka, Itsusei, *Traditional Kumihimo: Maru Dai*, Domyo, Tokyo, Japan, 1975

Shufuno, Tomosha and Yamaoka, Itsusei, *Traditional Kumihimo: Taka Dai and Taya Taka Dai*, Domyo, Tokyo, Japan, 1976

Tairyusha, *Kumihimo*, Tairyusha, Japan, 1978

Tairyusha, *Dyeing and Kumihimo* (special volume), Tairyusha, Japan, 1978

Tokoro, Hoko, *Traditional Craft of Kumihimo*, Chunichi Newspaper East, Nagoya, Japan, 1978

Tokoro, Hoko, *Kumihimo Plant Dyes*, Chunichi Newspaper East, Nagoya, Japan, 1980

Yamamot, Kaoru, *The Study of Kumihimo*, Sogo Gagaku, Tokyo, Japan, 1978

PERUVIAN SLING BRAIDING

Bellinger, Louisa and Bird, Junius, *Paracas Fabrics and Nazc Needlework*, The Textile Museum, USA, 1954

Cahlander, Adele, *Sling Braids of the Andes*, Colorado Fibre Centre, USA, 1980

D'Harcourt, Raoul, *Textiles of Ancient Peru and Their Techniques*, University of Washington, USA, 1962

Means, Philip A., *Distribution of Slings in Precolumbian America*, Proceedings of the National Museum of the United States, T507UN3P, vol. 55, USA, 1920

Montell, Gosta, *Dress and Ornaments in Ancient Peru*, Goteborg, Sweden, 1929

Noble, Carol R., *Peruvian Slings and their Regional Variation*, Weavers Journal, USA, Spring 1982

Paulin, Lynn, *Weaving on Rings and Hoops*, Gick Publishing Inc., USA, 1978

Zorn, Elayne, *Sling Braiding in the Macosani Area of Peru*, USA, 1980

HAIR BRAIDING

Andersen, Karen, *Karkullorna Fra Vanhus* (written in Danish), Denmark, 1984

Campbell, Mark, *The Art of Hairwork*, Lacis Publications, USA, 1984

OTHER REFERENCES

Aldridge, George, *Making Solid Sennits*, International Guild of Knot Tiers, UK

Anton, Ferdinand, *Ancient Peruvian Textiles*, Thames & Hudson, London, UK, 1987

Ashley, Clifford, *The Ashley Book of Knots*, Faber & Faber, London, UK, 1947

Collingwood, Peter, *Textile and Weaving Structures*, B.T. Batsford, London, UK, 1987

Cook, Lorraine, Court, Jean, Pound, Lynda, Stevenson, Judith and Wadsworth, John, *The Early Years Mathematics*, Harcourt Brace Jovanovich, London, UK, 1992

Crowfoot, Grace, 'Handicrafts in Palestine' in *Palestine Exploration Quarterly*, UK, July/October 1943

Hildburgh, W.L., 'Folklore' in *Folklore* vol. LV, UK, December 1944

Korfmann, Manfred, 'The Sling as a Weapon' in *Scientific American* vol. 229, no. 4, USA, October 1973

Larsen, Jack Lenor, *Interlacing: The Elemental Fabric*, Kodansha, Tokyo, Japan, and New York, USA, 1986

Murase, Miyeko, *The Arts of Japan*, McGraw Hill, London, UK, 1977

Storry, Richard, *The Way of the Samurai*, Orbis Publishing, London, UK, 1978

Turnbull, Stephen R., *The Book of the Samurai*, Bison Books, London, UK, 1982

Van der Post, Laurens, *Portrait of Japan*, Hogarth Press, London, UK, 1978

Yanagi, Soetsu, *The Unknown Craftsman*, Kodansha, Tokyo, Japan, 1972

Suppliers

Key: B = books, E = equipment, F = fittings, Y = yarns

UNITED KINGDOM

The Carey Company (B, E, F, Y)
75 Slade Close, Ottery St Mary, Devon EX11 1SY

Leanda (E)
D. J. Crisp
39 Borrowdale Drive, Norwich, Norfolk NR1 4LY

Edna Gibson (B, E, F)
70 Furzehatt Road, Plymstock, Plymouth, Devon PL9 8QT

CANADA

Shirley Berlin (E)
501 Langvista Drive, Victoria, British Columbia V9B 5J6

UNITED STATES

Charlene Marietti (E, B, Y)
Filamenti
2 Dickson Drive, Medford, New Jersey 08055

Lacis (B, Y)
3163 Adeline Street, Berkeley, California 94702

Things Japanese (Y)
9805N 116th Suite 7160, Kirkland, Washington 98034

The Weaver's Place
75 Mellor Avenue, Baltimore, Maryland 21228

Index

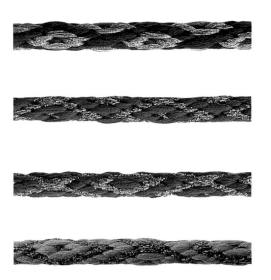